THE UK AIR FI COOKBOOK FOR BEGINNERS

365 days of Super-Delicious and Healthy Recipes for Family and Friends on a Budget

IRENE M. BASS

Copyright© 2022 By Irene M. Bass Rights Reserved

This book is copyright protected. It is only for personal use. You cannot amend, distribute, sell, use, quote or paraphrase any part of the content within this book, without the consent of the author or publisher.

Under no circumstances will any blame or legal responsibility be held against the publisher, or author, for any damages, reparation, or monetary loss due to the information contained within this book, either directly or indirectly.

Disclaimer Notice:

Please note the information contained within this document is for educational and entertainment purposes only. All effort has been executed to present accurate, up to date, reliable, complete information. No warranties of any kind are declared or implied. Readers acknowledge that the author is not engaged in the rendering of legal, financial, medical or professional advice. The content within this book has been derived from various sources. Please consult a licensed professional before attempting any techniques outlined in this book.

By reading this document, the reader agrees that under no circumstances is the author responsible for any losses, direct or indirect, that are incurred as a result of the use of the information contained within this document, including, but not limited to, errors, omissions, or inaccuracies.

Table of Contents

Introduction	1
Chapter 1	
Basics of UK Air Fryer	2
Foods to Enjoy with an Air Fryer	3
Advantages of Air Frying	4
Chapter 2	
Staples	5
Creamy Almond Glaze	6
Tartar Sauce	6
Garlicky banger Gravy	6
Chili Taco Seasoning	6
Classic Ranch Dressing	7
Creamy Blue Cheese Dressing	7
Homemade Tzatziki Sauce	7
Easy Pizza Dough	7
Air-Fried Hard-Boiled Eggs	8
Herb-Avocado Compound Butter	8
Strawberry-Coconut Butter	8
Oregano Balsamic Dressing	8
Lime Basil Dressing	9
Dijon Mayonnaise	9
Lemony Caesar Dressing	9
Classic Marinara Sauce	10
Enchilada Sauce	10
Roasted Mushrooms	11
Shawarma Spice Mix	11
Simple Teriyaki Sauce	11
Chapter 3	
Breakfast	12
Lean Turkey banger	13
Roma Tomato and Spinach Egg	13
Savory Mozzarella Bagels	14
Pork banger Egg Cup	14
Cheddar banger Meatball	14
Pork banger Cheese Biscuit	15
Turkey banger Burger with Avocado	15
Speedy Omelet	15
Soft Pita Breads	16
Tomato-Avocado Toast	16
Turkey-Mushroom Burger	17
Vegan Sandwich-Tofu with Cabbage	17
Muffins with Pecans and Kiwi	17
banger Eggs with Smoky Mustard Sauce	18
Nutty muesli	18
Chapter 4	
Poultry	19
Chicken and Bell Pepper Fajitas	20
Chicken Nuggets with Almond Crust	20
Chicken Cordon Bleu with Emmethaler	20
Curried Chicken with Orange and Honey	21
Chili-Garlic Chicken Tenders	21
Curried Cinnamon Chicken	22
Chicken Lettuce Tacos with Peanut Sauce	22

Curried Cranberry and Apple Chicken	23
Chicken Manchurian with Ketchup Sauce	23
Chicken and Cranberry Salad	24
Chicken Puttanesca	24
Chicken with Cucumber and Avocado Salad	25
Garlic-Chili Chicken	25
Cajun Chicken with Bell Peppers	26
Ground Chicken with Tomatoes	26
Crispy Chicken Strips	27
Chicken with Veggie Couscous Salad	27
Chicken Thighs with Mirin	28
Garlicky Whole Chicken Bake	28
Coriander Chicken with Lime	29
Garlic Chicken Wings	29
Chapter 5	
Fish and Seafood	30
Balsamic Tilapia	31
Crunchy Red Fish	31
Cumin Catfish	32
Blackened Salmon	32
Tender Tilapia	32
Rosemary Prawn Skewers	32
Sweet Tilapia Fillets	33
Balsamic Cod	33
Wrapped Scallops	33
Cod and Sauce	33
Thyme Catfish	34
Salmon and Creamy Chives Sauce	34
Garlic Prawn Mix	35
Tilapia and Tomato Salsa	35
Crusted Turmeric Salmon	36
Catfish with Spring Onions and Avocado	36
Ginger Cod	37
Paprika Tilapia	37
Prawn Skewers	38
Stevia Cod	38
Butter Crab Muffins	38
Tilapia and Kale	38
Chapter 6	
Pork, Beef, and Lamb	39
Roasted Peppery Loin	40
Sweet and Sour Meatballs	40
Greek-Style Pork Loin	41
Pork Bulgogi with Peppers	41
Roasted Chinese Five-Spice Pork Ribs	42
Roasted Boston Butt	42
Pork Cutlets with Plum Sauce	43
Yummy Chifa Chicharonnes	43
Pineapple-Pork Wrap	44
Pork Wontons	44
Pork Loin with Creamy Mushroom	45
Spicy Pork Ribs	45
Golden and Crisp Cod Fillets	46
Pork Chops with Applesauce	46
Steak with Butter	47

Steak with Bell Pepper	47
Garlicky Beef Roast	48
Cheesy Beef Burger with Mushroom	48
Beef Steak Shallots	49
Steak with Horseradish Cream	49
Sliced Peppery Pork	50
Super Easy Steak for Two	50

Chapter 7
Vegan and Vegetarian — 51

Bean, Salsa, and Cheese Tacos	52
Roasted Vegetables with Basil	52
Balsamic Asparagus	53
Mediterranean Baked Eggs with Spinach	53
Herbed Broccoli with Cheese	54
Cayenne Tahini Kale	54
Caramelized aubergine with Yogurt Sauce	55
Cheesy Cabbage Wedges	55
Air Fried Winter Vegetables	56
Rosemary Roasted marrow with Cheese	56
Asian-Inspired Broccoli	57
Roasted Brussels Sprouts with Parmesan	57
Creamy and Cheesy Spinach	58
Mascarpone Mushrooms	58
Spicy Cauliflower Roast	59
Italian Baked Tofu	59
Crispy Tofu Sticks	60
Tofu, Carrot and Cauliflower Rice	60

Chapter 8
Rice and Grains — 61

Cheesy Macaroni	62
Curry Basmati Rice	62
Chawal ke Pakore with Cheese	63
Eggy bread	63
Air Fried Butter Toast	64
Figs Bread Pudding	64
Rice with Scallions	65
Pecans Porridge Cups	65
Juicy Quinoa Porridge	66
Rice Cheese Casserole	66
Methi and Ragi Fritters	67
Doughnut Bread Pudding	67
Biryani with Butter	68
Chocolate Chips Honey Muffins	68
Baked Rolls with Cheese	69
Almonds Porridge	69
Chocolate Chips muesli	70
Cheesy Butter Macaroni	70
Blueberry Cheese Rolls	71
Pumpkin Porridge with Chocolate	71

Chapter 9
Starters and Snacks — 72

Avocado Chips	73
Baked Sardines with Tomato Sauce	73
Broiled Prosciutto-Wrapped Pears	74
Browned Ricotta with Capers and Lemon	74
Bruschetta with Tomato and Basil	75
Roasted Grapes with Yogurt	75
Roasted Mixed Nuts	76
Salty Baked Almonds	76

Banger and Mushroom Empanadas	77
banger and Onion Rolls	77
Banger Balls With Cheese	78
Prawn Toasts with Sesame Seeds	78
Tuna Melts with Scallions	79
Turkey Bacon-Wrapped Dates	79
Lemon Ricotta Cake	80
Lemon-Butter Shortbread	80
Lemon-Raspberry Muffins	81
Mixed Berries with Pecan Streusel Topping	81
Orange and Anise Cake	81

Appendix 1 Measurement Conversion Chart	82
Appendix 2 The Dirty Dozen and Clean Fifteen	83
Appendix 3 Index	84

Introduction

Are you unsure of what an air fryer is or whether you ought to purchase one?

You might be curious to learn more about air fryers if you've seen them in stores. Many people are unsure of what air fryers are, how they operate, and whether they are a helpful kitchen device due to the term's ambiguity and the apparent absurdity of frying food in air. Air fryers are the newest and best invention to the world of kitchen technologies, with merely the flow of hot air, this kitchen appliance can prepare your go-to meals. The air fryer is the kitchen device for you if you are often disappointed by the lack of crispiness in your meals. The crunch of french fries, the cracking of chicken wings, and the delicate, shattering surface and fluffy interior of doughnuts can all be achieved with the air fryer.

Chapter 1
Basics of UK Air Fryer

Air that has been heated is blown around the dish to produce a crunchy, crispy exterior. Air-fried foods are marketed as a healthier alternative to deep-fried ones since they contain less fat and calories.. Just a tablespoon (15 mL) of oil is needed to air-fry food to produce results that are similar to deep-fried items in terms of taste and texture. Now that you know that your air fryer is useful for more than simply fried and packaged dishes, read on. You're about to witness how, with just a little effort, you can create delicious, healthful foods from scratch with fresh ingredients.

Foods to Enjoy with an Air Fryer

Focus on consuming high-quality carbohydrates (mainly veggies), healthy fats, and lean proteins to maintain a well-balanced diet that can still help you lose weight. Fortunately, a terrific appliance for cooking a wide variety of dishes that fit into these categories is the air fryer.

VEGGIES

Almost every weight loss plan should include vegetables as a vital ingredient. In addition to being nutrient-dense and calorie-efficient, vegetables are also a great source of fiber, water, and other substances. They provide healthful carbs as well (more on that shortly).

The issue is that being sick of vegetables can happen quickly when we strive to consume exclusively healthy foods. We go into a rut where we only ever eat a few different foods. Instead of munching on carrot sticks, we find ourselves suddenly reaching for a bag of chips.

Long-term weight loss requires experimenting with delightful new vegetable preparations. Vegetables that have been air-fried can taste roasted and feel slightly crispy. Without using a ton of unneeded oil, these results are met. I adore the versatility of being able to air fry fresh vegetables without the need for pre-cooking. We almost always serve simple roasted cauliflower and smoky sweet potatoes.

APPROPRIATE FATS

In general, people think poorly of fat people. It's true that trans fats and saturated fats should be avoided, especially while trying to lose weight. Healthy fats, however, are also essential for our bodies' ability to create certain hormones, stimulate cell growth, absorb certain nutrients, and produce energy.
Good fats include monounsaturated and polyunsaturated fats. Avocados, almonds, seeds, and fish are a few frequent foods that are high in healthy fats. Additionally, some oils have lower saturated fat content, they're more desirable since they're obese. Avocado, canola, corn, olive, grapeseed, safflower, peanut, sesame, soybean, and sunflower oils are the least saturated fat-containing ones.

When I need to use oil to prepare food in the air fryer, I usually use an olive oil spray. For air frying, very little oil is needed. Olive oil can be used sparingly to give food the crispy texture we love in fried foods without adding the same amount of calories as typical deep-frying.

LEAN PROTEINS

If you don't feel hungry, you won't be tempted to snack or eat as much at your next meal because protein keeps you satisfied for longer. The assistance protein provides your body in preserving lean muscle mass is another advantage.

But not all proteins are made equal. Some protein sources, such as fatty meat cuts, hot dogs, bacon, and other processed meats, are highly high in saturated fat. If you're attempting to reduce weight, it's crucial to choose lean proteins. When making meal plans, choose turkey, chicken, and lean beef and hog chops.

Just a few of the cookbook's protein-rich recipes include Lemon-Garlic Tilapia, Whole Roasted Chicken, and Easy Turkey Tenderloin.

Ghrelin, the hunger hormone, is known to be decreased by protein, while levels of the peptide YY, which makes you feel full, are increased.

EXCEPTIONAL CARBOHYDRATES

Sweet potatoes and potatoes seem to be contentious veggies when it comes to losing weight. These potatoes are both incredibly nutrient-dense. They contain a lot of fiber and the vitamins B6 and C. The position of these potatoes on the glycemic index varies. Compared to typical white potatoes, sweet potatoes have a lower glycemic index. The many benefits of potatoes can speed up your feeling of fullness. It's important to serve them alongside lean protein rather than slathering them in butter or other fatty sauces.

Other foods that include high-quality carbs outside vegetables include fruits, whole grains, plantains, beans and other legumes. They not only contain a wealth of vitamins and minerals, but also assist in stabilizing our blood sugar levels and prevent changes in our levels of insulin.

After a blood-sugar increase, it's typical to feel hungry and overeat. These increases can be brought on by low-quality carbs found in processed foods, white bread, sweets, juices, and other sugary beverages. Eating a diet rich in processed, low-quality carbs makes it exceedingly difficult to lose weight.

I don't feel at all deprived because I've found scrumptious alternatives to highly processed carbohydrates. Zucchini noodles can be used in place of spaghetti noodles, and riced cauliflower can be used in place of white rice. I use the air fryer to transform high-quality, basic carbs into delicious meals that my entire family adores. The best thing is that I am preparing meals with whole foods that are rich in the nutrients my body needs.

Advantages of Air Frying

The following are the health advantages of using an air fryer properly:

- Reduces intake of unhealthy oils on a regular basis and switching from deep-fried to air-fried dishes can both help you lose weight.
- Oesophageal, endometrial, ovarian, pancreatic, and breast cancers, among others, may all be related to hazardous acrylamide production, according to the International Agency for Research on Cancer.
- People can reduce the possibility that acrylamide will be present in their meals by switching to air frying.
- Lowers the chance of illness
- Traditional fried foods and oil-based cooking have been linked to a variety of harmful health issues. A person's chance of developing these issues can be decreased by using alternate cooking techniques for deep frying.

Chapter 2
Staples

Creamy Almond Glaze

Prep time: 5 minutes | Cook time: 0 minutes | Serves 8

- ½ cup Swerve
- ½ tablespoon unsalted butter, at room temperature
- 2 to 3 tablespoons heavy (whipping) cream
- ¼ teaspoon almond extract
- ¼ teaspoon pure vanilla extract

1. Combine the Swerve, butter, 2 tablespoons of double cream, almond extract, and vanilla extract in a large bowl. Whisk until creamy, adding additional double cream as needed to achieve your preferred consistency.
2. Drizzle over cinnamon rolls, blueberry muffins, or biscuits.

Tartar Sauce

Prep time: 5 minutes | Cook time: 0 minutes | Serves 8

- ½ cup sugar-free mayonnaise
- ¼ cup diced dill pickles
- 1 shallot, diced
- 2 tablespoons drained capers, rinsed and chopped
- 2 teaspoons Swerve
- 2 teaspoons dill pickle juice
- 1 teaspoon dried dill
- ½ teaspoon sea salt
- ½ teaspoon freshly ground black pepper
- ⅛ teaspoon cayenne pepper

1. In a medium bowl, mix together the mayonnaise, pickles, shallot, capers, Swerve, pickle juice, dill, salt, pepper, and cayenne pepper until thoroughly combined.
2. Cover and refrigerate until ready to serve.

Garlicky banger Gravy

Prep time: 10 minutes | Cook time: 13 minutes | Serves 8

- 1 tablespoon unsalted butter
- 12 ounces (340 g) breakfast banger, casings removed
- ⅓ cup chopped onion
- 1 cup chicken broth
- 1 cup heavy (whipping) cream
- 8 ounces (227 g) cream cheese, cut into cubes
- ¼ teaspoon xanthan gum
- 1½ teaspoons garlic powder
- ½ teaspoon sea salt
- ½ teaspoon freshly ground black pepper

1. Melt the butter in a large saucepan over medium-high heat. Add the banger and cook, using a spoon to break up the meat, for about 6 minutes or until the banger is no longer pink. Add the onion and cook for 2 minutes. Stir in the broth, double cream, cream cheese, and xanthan gum.
2. Bring the mixture to a simmer, whisking constantly. Reduce the heat to medium-low and cook until the mixture thickens, about 5 minutes.
3. Stir in the garlic powder, salt, and pepper; serve hot.

Chili Taco Seasoning

Prep time: 5 minutes | Cook time: 0 minutes | Serves 8

- 3 tablespoons chili powder
- 1½ tablespoons ground cumin
- 1½ tablespoons garlic powder
- 1 tablespoon sea salt
- 2 teaspoons onion powder
- 2 teaspoons smoked paprika
- 2 teaspoons dried oregano
- 1 teaspoon freshly ground black pepper
- ¼ teaspoon cayenne pepper

1. In a small bowl, combine the chili powder, cumin, garlic powder, salt, onion powder, smoked paprika, oregano, black pepper, and cayenne pepper.
2. Transfer to a small, airtight jar, seal, and store in your pantry.

Classic Ranch Dressing
Prep time: 10 minutes | Cook time: 0 minutes | Serves 12

- ¼ cup heavy (whipping) cream
- 1 teaspoon apple cider vinegar
- ½ cup sugar-free mayonnaise
- ½ cup Soured cream
- 1 tablespoon minced garlic
- 1 teaspoon dried oregano
- 1 teaspoon onion powder
- 1 teaspoon sea salt
- ½ teaspoon dried dill
- ½ teaspoon freshly ground black pepper
- Additional double cream or bone broth, for thinning

1. Whisk together the double cream and apple cider vinegar in a medium bowl until combined. Let the mixture rest for 10 minutes, then whisk in the mayonnaise, Soured cream, garlic, oregano, onion powder, salt, dill, and pepper.
2. Thin the dressing to your desired consistency, using more double cream or bone broth (it will no longer be vegetarian if you use bone broth).
3. Transfer to an airtight container, and refrigerate for up to 1 week.

Creamy Blue Cheese Dressing
Prep time: 5 minutes | Cook time: 0 minutes | Serves 12

- ¾ cup sugar-free mayonnaise
- ¼ cup Soured cream
- ½ cup heavy (whipping) cream
- 1 teaspoon minced garlic
- 1 tablespoon freshly squeezed lemon juice
- 1 tablespoon apple cider vinegar
- 1 teaspoon chili sauce
- ½ teaspoon sea salt
- 4 ounces (113 g) blue cheese, crumbled (about ¾ cup)

1. In a medium bowl, whisk together the mayonnaise, Soured cream, and double cream.
2. Stir in the garlic, lemon juice, apple cider vinegar, chili sauce, and sea salt.
3. Add the blue cheese crumbles, and stir until well combined.
4. Transfer to an airtight container, and refrigerate for up to 1 week.

Homemade Tzatziki Sauce
Prep time: 15 minutes | Cook time: 0 minutes | Serves 6

- ½ cucumber, seeded and finely chopped
- ½ teaspoon sea salt, plus additional for seasoning
- ¾ cup Soured cream
- 1 tablespoon freshly squeezed lemon juice
- 1 tablespoon chopped fresh dill
- 3 garlic cloves, minced

1. Place the cucumber in a colander set in the sink or over a bowl, and sprinkle it with salt. Let stand for 10 minutes, then transfer the cucumber to a clean dishcloth and wring it out, extracting as much liquid as you can.
2. In a medium bowl, stir together the cucumber, Soured cream, lemon juice, dill, garlic, and ½ teaspoon of salt.
3. Store the sauce in an airtight container in the refrigerator for up to 4 days.

Easy Pizza Dough
Prep time: 10 minutes | Cook time: 0 minutes | Serves 8

- 6 ounces (170 g) low-moisture Mozzarella cheese, shredded (about 1½ cups)
- 2 ounces (57 g) cream cheese, diced
- 1 large egg
- 1 cup finely ground blanched almond flour
- ½ teaspoon sea salt
- ¼ teaspoon freshly ground black pepper

1. Combine the Mozzarella cheese and cream cheese in a medium saucepan over medium heat. Cook, stirring often, until the cheeses are melted.
2. Remove the pan from the heat and stir in the egg, almond flour, salt, and pepper.
3. Transfer the mixture to a sheet of greaseproof paper and knead the dough until it is well combined.
4. Place the dough between 2 sheets of greaseproof paper. Roll out the dough to your preferred thickness (or whatever thickness your recipe requires). Cook as directed to make pizza, calzones, or empanadas.

Air-Fried Hard-Boiled Eggs

Prep time: 2 minutes | Cook time: 18 minutes | Serves 4

- 4 large eggs
- 1 cup water

1. Place eggs into a 4-cup round baking-safe dish and pour water over eggs. Place dish into the air fryer basket or wire rack.
2. Adjust the temperature to 150°C and air fry for 18 minutes.
3. Store cooked eggs in the refrigerator until ready to use or peel and eat warm.

Herb Avocado Compound Butter

Prep time: 25 minutes | Cook time: 0 minutes | Makes 2 cups

- ¼ cup butter, at room temperature
- 1 avocado, peeled, pitted, and cut into quarters
- Juice of ½ lemon
- 2 teaspoons chopped Coriander
- 1 teaspoon chopped fresh basil
- 1 teaspoon minced garlic
- Sea salt and freshly ground black pepper, to taste

1. Place the butter, avocado, lemon juice, Coriander, basil, and garlic in a food processor and process until smooth.
2. Season the butter with salt and pepper.
3. Transfer the mixture to a sheet of greaseproof paper and shape it into a log.
4. Place the parchment butter log in the refrigerator until it is firm, about 4 hours.
5. Serve slices of this butter with fish or chicken.
6. Store unused butter wrapped tightly in the freezer for up to 1 week.

Strawberry-Coconut Butter

Prep time: 25 minutes | Cook time: 0 minutes | Makes 3 cups

- 2 cups shredded unsweetened coconut
- 1 tablespoon coconut oil
- ¾ cup fresh strawberries
- ½ tablespoon freshly squeezed lemon juice
- 1 teaspoon alcohol-free pure vanilla extract

1. Put the coconut in a food processor and purée it until it is buttery and smooth, about 15 minutes.
2. Add the coconut oil, strawberries, lemon juice, and vanilla to the coconut butter and process until very smooth, scraping down the sides of the bowl.
3. Pass the butter through a fine sieve to remove the strawberry seeds, using the back of a spoon to press the butter through.
4. Store the strawberry butter in an airtight container in the refrigerator for up to 2 weeks.
5. Serve chicken or fish with a spoon of this butter on top.

Oregano Balsamic Dressing

Prep time: 4 minutes | Cook time: 0 minutes | Makes 1 cup

- 1 cup extra-virgin olive oil
- ¼ cup balsamic vinegar
- 2 tablespoons chopped fresh oregano
- 1 teaspoon chopped fresh basil
- 1 teaspoon minced garlic
- Sea salt and freshly ground black pepper, to taste

1. Whisk the olive oil and vinegar in a small bowl until emulsified, about 3 minutes.
2. Whisk in the oregano, basil, and garlic until well combined, about 1 minute.
3. Season the dressing with salt and pepper.
4. Transfer the dressing to an airtight container, and store it in the refrigerator for up to 1 week. Give the dressing a vigorous shake before using it.

Lime Basil Dressing
Prep time: 10 minutes | Cook time: 0 minutes | Makes 1 cup

- 1 avocado, peeled and pitted
- ¼ cup Soured cream
- ¼ cup extra-virgin olive oil
- ¼ cup chopped fresh basil
- 1 tablespoon freshly squeezed lime juice
- 1 teaspoon minced garlic
- Sea salt and freshly ground black pepper, to taste

1. Place the avocado, Soured cream, olive oil, basil, lime juice, and garlic in a food processor and pulse until smooth, scraping down the sides of the bowl once during processing.
2. Season the dressing with salt and pepper.
3. Keep the dressing in an airtight container in the refrigerator for 1 to 2 weeks.

Dijon Mayonnaise
Prep time: 10 minutes | Cook time: 0 minutes | Makes 4 cups

- 2 large eggs
- 2 tablespoons Dijon mustard
- 1½ cups extra-virgin olive oil
- ¼ cup freshly squeezed lemon juice
- Sea salt and freshly ground black pepper, to taste

1. Whisk the eggs and mustard together in a heavy, large bowl until very well combined, about 2 minutes.
2. Add the oil in a continuous thin stream, whisking constantly, until the mayonnaise is thick and completely emulsified.
3. Add the lemon juice and whisk until well blended.
4. Season with salt and pepper.

Lemony Caesar Dressing
Prep time: 10 minutes | Cook time: 5 minutes | Makes 1½ cups

- 2 teaspoons minced garlic
- 4 large egg yolks
- ¼ cup wine vinegar
- ½ teaspoon dry mustard
- Dash Worcestershire sauce
- 1 cup extra-virgin olive oil
- ¼ cup freshly squeezed lemon juice
- Sea salt and freshly ground black pepper, to taste

1. To a small saucepan, add the garlic, egg yolks, vinegar, mustard, and Worcestershire sauce and place over low heat.
2. Whisking constantly, cook the mixture until it thickens and is a little bubbly, about 5 minutes.
3. Remove from saucepan from the heat and let it stand for about 10 minutes to cool.
4. Transfer the egg mixture to a large stainless steel bowl. Whisking constantly, add the olive oil in a thin stream.
5. Whisk in the lemon juice and season the dressing with salt and pepper.
6. Transfer the dressing to an airtight container and keep in the refrigerator for up to 3 days.

Classic Marinara Sauce

Prep time: 15 minutes | Cook time: 30 minutes | Makes about 3 cups

- ¼ cup extra-virgin olive oil
- 3 garlic cloves, minced
- 1 small onion, chopped (about ½ cup)
- 2 tablespoons minced or puréed sun-dried tomatoes (optional)
- 1 (28-ounce / 794-g) can crushed tomatoes
- ½ teaspoon dried basil
- ½ teaspoon dried oregano
- ¼ teaspoon red pepper flakes
- 1 teaspoon flake salt or ½ teaspoon fine salt, plus more as needed

1. Heat the oil in a medium saucepan over medium heat.
2. Add the garlic and onion and sauté for 2 to 3 minutes, or until the onion is softened. Add the sun-dried tomatoes (if desired) and cook for 1 minute until fragrant. Stir in the crushed tomatoes, scraping any brown bits from the bottom of the pot. Fold in the basil, oregano, red pepper flakes, and salt. Stir well.
3. Bring to a simmer. Cook covered for about 30 minutes, stirring occasionally.
4. Turn off the heat and allow the sauce to cool for about 10 minutes.
5. Taste and adjust the seasoning, adding more salt if needed.
6. Use immediately.

Enchilada Sauce

Prep time: 15 minutes | Cook time: 0 minutes | Makes 2 cups

- 3 large ancho chiles, stems and seeds removed, torn into pieces
- 1½ cups very hot water
- 2 garlic cloves, peeled and lightly smashed
- 2 tablespoons wine vinegar
- 1½ teaspoons sugar
- ½ teaspoon dried oregano
- ½ teaspoon ground cumin
- 2 teaspoons flake salt or 1 teaspoon fine salt

1. Mix together the chile pieces and hot water in a bowl and let stand for 10 to 15 minutes.
2. Pour the chiles and water into a blender jar. Fold in the garlic, vinegar, sugar, oregano, cumin, and salt and blend until smooth.
3. Use immediately.

Roasted Mushrooms

Prep time: 8 minutes | Cook time: 30 minutes | Makes about 1½ cups

- 1 pound (454 g) button or cremini mushrooms, washed, stems trimmed, and cut into quarters or thick slices
- ¼ cup water
- 1 teaspoon flake salt or ½ teaspoon fine salt
- 3 tablespoons unsalted butter, cut into pieces, or extra-virgin olive oil

1. Place a large piece of tin foil on a sheet pan. Place the mushroom pieces in the middle of the foil. Spread them out into an even layer. Pour the water over them, season with the salt, and add the butter. Wrap the mushrooms in the foil.
2. Press the Power Button. Cook at 160°C for 15 minutes.
3. After 15 minutes, remove from the air fryer oven. Transfer the foil packet to a cutting board and carefully unwrap it. Pour the mushrooms and cooking liquid from the foil onto the sheet pan.
4. Return the pan to the air fryer oven. Press the Power Button. Cook at 180°C for 15 minutes.
5. After about 10 minutes, remove from the air fryer oven and stir the mushrooms. Return to the air fryer oven and continue cooking for anywhere from 5 to 15 more minutes, or until the liquid is mostly gone and the mushrooms start to brown.
6. Serve immediately.

Shawarma Spice Mix

Prep time: 5 minutes | Cook time: 0 minutes | Makes about 1 tablespoon

- 1 teaspoon smoked paprika
- 1 teaspoon cumin
- ¼ teaspoon turmeric
- ¼ teaspoon flake salt or ⅛ teaspoon fine salt
- ¼ teaspoon cinnamon
- ¼ teaspoon allspice
- ¼ teaspoon red pepper flakes
- ¼ teaspoon freshly ground black pepper

1. Stir together all the ingredients in a small bowl.
2. Use immediately or place in an airtight container in the pantry.

Simple Teriyaki Sauce

Prep time: 5 minutes | Cook time: 0 minutes | Makes ¾ cup

- ½ cup soy sauce
- 3 tablespoons honey
- 1 tablespoon rice wine or dry sherry
- 1 tablespoon rice vinegar
- 2 teaspoons minced fresh ginger
- 2 garlic cloves, smashed

1. Beat together all the ingredients in a small bowl.
2. Use immediately.

Chapter 3
Breakfast

Lean Turkey banger

Prep time: 15 minutes | Cook time: 20 minutes | Serves 8

- 1½ pounds (680g) 85% lean ground turkey
- 3 cloves garlic, finely chopped
- ¼ onion, grated
- 1 teaspoon Tabasco sauce
- 1 teaspoon Cajun seasoning
- 1 teaspoon dried thyme
- ½ teaspoon paprika
- ½ teaspoon cayenne

1. Preheat the air fryer to 190°C.
2. In a large bowl, combine the turkey, garlic, onion, Tabasco, Cajun seasoning, thyme, paprika, and cayenne. Mix with clean hands until thoroughly combined. Shape into 16 patties, about ½ -inch thick. (Wet your hands slightly if you find the banger too sticky to handle.)
3. Working in batches if necessary, arrange the patties in a single layer in the air fryer basket or wire rack. Pausing halfway through the cooking time to flip the patties, air fry for 15 to 20 minutes until a thermometer inserted into the thickest portion registers 165°F (74°C).

Roma Tomato and Spinach Egg

Prep time: 10 minutes | Cook time: 15 minutes | Serves 4T

- 2 cups 100% liquid egg whites
- 3 tablespoons salted butter, melted
- ¼ teaspoon salt
- ¼ teaspoon onion powder
- ½ medium Roma tomato, cored and diced
- ½ cup chopped fresh spinach leaves

1. In a large bowl, whisk egg whites with butter, salt, and onion powder. Stir in tomato and spinach, then pour evenly into four 4-inch ramekins greased with cooking spray.
2. Place ramekins into air fryer basket or wire rack. Adjust the temperature to 150°C 150°C and set the timer for 15 minutes. Eggs will be fully cooked and firm in the center when done. Serve warm.

Savory Mozzarella Bagels

Prep time: 15 minutes | Cook time: 14 minutes | Serves 6

- 1¾ cups shredded Mozzarella cheese or goat cheese
- 2 tablespoons unsalted butter or coconut oil
- 1 large egg, beaten
- 1 tablespoon apple cider vinegar
- 1 cup blanched almond flour
- 1 tablespoon baking powder
- ⅛ teaspoon fine sea salt
- 1½ teaspoons everything bagel seasoning

1. Make the dough: Put the Mozzarella and butter in a large microwave-safe bowl and microwave for 1 to 2 minutes, until the cheese is entirely melted. Stir well. Add the egg and vinegar. Using a hand mixer on medium, combine well. Add the almond flour, baking powder, and salt and, using the mixer, combine well.
2. Lay a piece of greaseproof paper on the countertop and place the dough on it. Knead it for about 3 minutes. The dough should be a little sticky but pliable. (If the dough is too sticky, chill it in the refrigerator for an hour or overnight.)
3. Preheat the air fryer to 180°C. Spray a baking tray or pie pan that will fit into your air fryer with avocado oil.
4. Divide the dough into 6 equal portions. Roll 1 portion into a log that is 6-inches long and about ½-inch thick. Form the log into a circle and seal the edges together, making a bagel shape. Repeat with the remaining portions of dough, making 6 bagels.
5. Place the bagels on the greased baking tray. Spray the bagels with avocado oil and top with everything bagel seasoning, pressing the seasoning into the dough with your hands.
6. Place the bagels in the air fryer and cook for 14 minutes, or until cooked through and golden brown, flipping after 6 minutes.
7. Remove the bagels from the air fryer and allow them to cool slightly before slicing them in half and serving. Store leftovers in an airtight container in the fridge for up to 4 days or in the freezer for up to a month.

Pork banger Egg Cup

Prep time: 10 minutes | Cook time: 15 minutes | Serves 6

- 12 ounces (340 g) ground pork breakfast banger
- 6 large eggs
- ½ teaspoon salt
- ¼ teaspoon ground black pepper
- ½ teaspoon crushed red pepper flakes

1. Place banger in six 4-inch ramekins (about 2 ounces (57 g) per ramekin) greased with cooking oil. Press banger down to cover bottom and about ½-inch up the sides of ramekins. Crack one egg into each ramekin and sprinkle evenly with salt, black pepper, and red pepper flakes.
2. Place ramekins into air fryer basket or wire rack. Adjust the temperature to 180°C and set the timer for 15 minutes. Egg cups will be done when banger is fully cooked to at least 145°F (63°C) and the egg is firm. Serve warm.

Cheddar banger Meatball

Prep time: 10 minutes | Cook time: 15 minutes | Serves 18 meatballs

- 1 pound (454 g) ground pork breakfast banger
- ½ teaspoon salt
- ¼ teaspoon ground black pepper
- ½ cup shredded sharp Cheddar cheese
- 1 ounce (28 g) cream cheese, softened
- 1 large egg, whisked

1. Combine all ingredients in a large bowl. Form mixture into eighteen 1-inch meatballs.
2. Place meatballs into ungreased air fryer basket or wire rack. Adjust the temperature to 200°C and set the timer for 15 minutes, shaking basket three times during cooking. Meatballs will be browned on the outside and have an internal temperature of at least 145°F (63°C) when completely cooked. Serve warm.

Pork banger Cheese Biscuit

Prep time: 20 minutes | Cook time: 30 minutes | Serves 4

FILLING:

- 10 ounces (283 g) bulk pork banger, crumbled
- ¼ cup minced onions
- 2 cloves garlic, minced
- ½ teaspoon fine sea salt
- ½ teaspoon ground black pepper
- 1 (8-ounce / 227-g) package cream cheese (or Kite Hill brand cream cheese style spread for dairy-free), softened
- ¾ cup beef or chicken broth
- Biscuits:
- 3 large egg whites
- ¾ cup blanched almond flour
- 1 teaspoon baking powder
- ¼ teaspoon fine sea salt
- 2½ tablespoons very cold unsalted butter, cut into ¼-inch pieces
- Fresh thyme leaves, for garnish

1. Preheat the air fryer to 200°C.
2. Place the banger, onions, and garlic in a 7-inch pie pan. Using your hands, break up the banger into small pieces and spread it evenly throughout the pie pan. Season with the salt and pepper. Place the pan in the air fryer and cook for 5 minutes.
3. While the banger cooks, place the cream cheese and broth in a food processor or blender and purée until smooth.
4. Remove the pork from the air fryer and use a fork or metal spatula to crumble it more. Pour the cream cheese mixture into the banger and stir to combine. Set aside.
5. Make the biscuits: Place the egg whites in a medium-sized mixing bowl or the bowl of a stand mixer and whip with a hand mixer or stand mixer until stiff peaks form.
6. In a separate medium-sized bowl, whisk together the almond flour, baking powder, and salt, then cut in the butter. When you are done, the mixture should still have chunks of butter. Gently fold the flour mixture into the egg whites with a rubber spatula.
7. Use a large spoon or ice cream scoop to scoop the dough into 4 equal-sized biscuits, making sure the butter is evenly distributed. Place the biscuits on top of the banger and cook in the air fryer for 5 minutes, then turn the heat down to 325°F (163°C) and cook for another 17 to 20 minutes, until the biscuits are golden brown. Serve garnished with fresh thyme leaves.
8. Store leftovers in an airtight container in the refrigerator for up to 3 days. Reheat in a preheated 180°C air fryer for 5 minutes, or until warmed through.

Turkey banger Burger with Avocado

Prep time: 5 minutes | Cook time: 15 minutes | Serves 4

- 1 pound (454 g) ground turkey breakfast banger
- ½ teaspoon salt
- ¼ teaspoon ground black pepper
- ¼ cup seeded and chopped green bell pepper
- 2 tablespoons mayonnaise
- 1 medium avocado, peeled, pitted, and sliced

1. In a large bowl, mix banger with salt, black pepper, bell pepper, and mayonnaise. Form meat into four patties.
2. Place patties into ungreased air fryer basket or wire rack. Adjust the temperature to 370°F and set the timer for 15 minutes, turning patties halfway through cooking. Burgers will be done when dark brown and they have an internal temperature of at least 165°F (74°C).
3. Serve burgers topped with avocado slices on four medium plates.

Speedy Omelet

Prep time: 5 minutes | Cook time: 15 minutes | Serves 2

- 3 large eggs
- 1 tablespoon salted butter, melted
- ¼ cup seeded and chopped green bell pepper
- 2 tablespoons peeled and chopped yellow onion
- ¼ cup chopped cooked no-sugar-added ham
- ¼ teaspoon salt
- ¼ teaspoon ground black pepper

1. Crack eggs into an ungreased 6-inch round nonstick baking dish. Mix in butter, bell pepper, onion, ham, salt, and black pepper.
2. Place dish into air fryer basket or wire rack. Adjust the temperature to 320°F (160°C) and set the timer for 15 minutes. The eggs will be fully cooked and firm in the middle when done.
3. Slice in half and serve warm on two medium plates.

Soft Pita Breads

Prep time: 10 minutes | Cook time: 6 minutes | Serves 8 mini pitas

- 2 teaspoons active dry yeast
- 1 tablespoon sugar
- 1¼ to 1½ cups warm water (90°F - 110°F)
- 3¼ cups plain flour
- 2 teaspoons salt
- 1 tablespoon olive oil, plus more for brushing
- flake salt(optional)

1. Dissolve the yeast, sugar and water in the bowl of a stand mixer. Let the mixture sit for 5 minutes to make sure the yeast is active – it should foam a little. (If there's no foaming, discard and start again with new yeast.) Combine the flour and salt in a bowl, and add it to the water, along with the olive oil. Mix with the dough hook until combined. Add a little more flour if needed to get the dough to pull away from the sides of the mixing bowl, or add a little more water if the dough seems too dry.
2. Knead the dough until it is smooth and elastic (about 8 minutes in the mixer or 15 minutes by hand). Transfer the dough to a lightly oiled bowl, cover and let it rise in a warm place until doubled in bulk.
3. Divide the dough into 8 portions and roll each portion into a circle about 4-inches in diameter. Don't roll the balls too thin, or you won't get the pocket inside the pita.
4. Pre-heat the air fryer to 200°C.
5. Brush both sides of the dough with olive oil, and sprinkle with flake saltif desired. Air-fry one at a time at 200°C for 6 minutes, flipping it over when there are two minutes left in the cooking time.

Tomato-Avocado Toast

Prep time: 5 minutes | Cook time: 0 minutes | Serves 2

- 2 slices thick whole grain bread
- 4 thin tomato slices
- 1 ripe avocado, pitted, peeled, and sliced
- 1 tablespoon olive oil
- 1 tablespoon pinch of salt
- ½ teaspoon chili flakes

1. Preheat air fryer to 190°C. Arrange the bread slices on the fryer and toast on Bake mode. Add the avocado to a bowl and mash it up with a fork until smooth. Season with salt.
2. When the toasted bread is ready, remove it to a plate. Drizzle with olive oil and arrange the thin tomato slices on top. Spread the avocado mash on top. Sprinkle the toasts with chili flakes and serve

Turkey-Mushroom Burger

Prep time: 10 minutes | Cook time: 0 minutes | Serves 1

- ⅓ cup leftover turkey, shredded
- ⅓ cup sliced mushrooms, sauteed
- ½ tablespoon butter, softened
- 2 tomato slices
- ½ teaspoon red pepper flakes
- Salt and black pepper to taste
- 1 bap, halved

1. Preheat air fryer to 180°C. Brush the bottom half with butter and top with shredded turkey.
2. Arrange mushroom slices on top of the turkey. Cover with tomato slices and sprinkle with salt, black pepper, and red flakes.
3. Top with the other bun half and Air Fry in the fryer for 5 to 8 minutes until crispy.

Vegan Sandwich-Tofu with Cabbage

Prep time: 5 minutes | Cook time: 8 minutes | Serves 1

- 2 slices of bread
- 1 slice tofu, 1-inch thick
- ¼ cup red cabbage, shredded
- 2 teaspoon olive oil
- ¼ teaspoon vinegar
- Salt and black pepper to taste

1. Preheat air fryer to 180°C. Add the bread slices to the air fryer basket or wire rack and toast for 3 minutes; set aside. Brush the tofu with some olive oil and place in the air fryer to Bake for 5 minutes on each side.
2. Mix the cabbage, remaining olive oil, and vinegar. Season with salt. Place the tofu on top of one bread slice, place the cabbage over, and top with the other bread slice. Serve with cream cheese-mustard dip.

Muffins with Pecans and Kiwi

Prep time: 10 minutes | Cook time: 15 minutes | Serves 4

- 1 cup flour
- 1 kiwi, mashed
- ¼ cup icing sugar
- 1 teaspoon milk
- 1 tablespoon pecans, chopped
- ½ teaspoon baking powder
- ¼ cup oats
- ¼ cup butter, room temperature

1. Preheat air fryer to 180°C. Place the sugar, pecans, kiwi, and butter in a bowl and mix well. In another bowl, mix the flour, baking powder, and oats and stir well. Combine the two mixtures and stir in the milk.
2. Pour the batter into a greased muffin tin that fits in the fryer and bake for 15 minutes. Remove to a wire rack and leave to cool for a few minutes before removing from the muffin tin. Enjoy!

Banger Eggs with Smoky Mustard Sauce

Prep time: 20 minutes | Cook time: 12 minutes | Serves 8

- 1 pound (454 g) pork banger
- 8 soft-boiled or hard-boiled eggs, peeled
- 1 large egg
- 2 tablespoons milk
- 1 cup crushed scratchings
- Smoky Mustard Sauce:
- ¼ cup mayonnaise
- 2 tablespoons Soured cream
- 1 tablespoon Dijon mustard
- 1 teaspoon chipotle chili sauce

1. Preheat the air fryer to 200°C.
2. Divide the banger into 8 portions. Take each portion of banger, pat it down into a patty, and place 1 egg in the middle, gently wrapping the banger around the egg until the egg is completely covered. (Wet your hands slightly if you find the banger to be too sticky.) Repeat with the remaining eggs and banger.
3. In a small shallow bowl, whisk the egg and milk until frothy. In another shallow bowl, place the crushed scratchings. Working one at a time, dip a banger-wrapped egg into the beaten egg and then into the scratchings, gently rolling to coat evenly. Repeat with the remaining banger-wrapped eggs.
4. Arrange the eggs in a single layer in the air fryer basket or wire rack, and lightly spray with olive oil. Air fry for 10 to 12 minutes, pausing halfway through the baking time to turn the eggs, until the eggs are hot and the banger is cooked through.
5. To make the sauce: In a small bowl, combine the mayonnaise, Soured cream, Dijon, and chili sauce. Whisk until thoroughly combined. Serve with the Scotch eggs.

Nutty muesli

Prep time: 10 minutes | Cook time: 5 minutes | Serves 6

- 2 cups pecans, chopped
- 1 cup unsweetened coconut flakes
- 1 cup almond slivers
- ⅓ cup sunflower seeds
- ¼ cup golden flaxseed
- ¼ cup low-carb, sugar-free chocolate chips
- ¼ cup granular erythritol
- 2 tablespoons unsalted butter
- 1 teaspoon ground cinnamon

1. In a large bowl, mix all ingredients.
2. Place the mixture into a 4-cup round baking dish. Place dish into the air fryer basket or wire rack.
3. Adjust the temperature to 320°F (160°C) and set the timer for 5 minutes.
4. Allow to cool completely before serving.

Chapter 4
Poultry

Chicken and Bell Pepper Fajitas

Prep time: 15 minutes | Cook time: 10 to 15 minutes | Serves 4

- 4 (5-ounce / 142-g) low-sodium boneless, skinless chicken breasts, cut into 4-by-½-inch strips
- 1 tablespoon freshly squeezed lemon juice
- 2 teaspoons olive oil
- 2 teaspoons chili powder
- 2 red bell peppers, sliced
- 4 low-sodium whole-wheat tortillas
- ⅓ cup nonfat Soured cream
- 1 cup grape tomatoes, sliced

1. Preheat the air fryer to 190°C.
2. In a large bowl, mix the chicken, lemon juice, olive oil, and chili powder. Toss to coat. Transfer the chicken to the baking pan. Add the red bell peppers. Bake for 10 to 15 minutes, or until the chicken reaches an internal temperature of 75°C on a meat thermometer.
3. Assemble the fajitas with the tortillas, chicken, bell peppers, Soured cream, and tomatoes. Serve immediately.

Chicken Nuggets with Almond Crust

Prep time: 10 minutes | Cook time: 10 to 13 minutes | Serves 4

- 1 egg white
- 1 tablespoon freshly squeezed lemon juice
- ½ teaspoon dried basil
- ½ teaspoon ground paprika
- 1 pound (454 g) low-sodium boneless, skinless chicken breasts, cut into 1½-inch cubes
- ½ cup ground almonds
- 2 slices low-sodium whole-wheat bread, crumbled

1. Preheat the air fryer to 200°C.
2. In a shallow bowl, beat the egg white, lemon juice, basil, and paprika with a fork until foamy.
3. Add the chicken and stir to coat.
4. On a plate, mix the almonds and bread crumbs.
5. Toss the chicken cubes in the almond and bread crumb mixture until coated.
6. Bake the nuggets in the air fryer, in two batches, for 10 to 13 minutes, or until the chicken reaches an internal temperature of 75°C on a meat thermometer. Serve immediately.

Chicken Cordon Bleu with Emmethaler

Prep time: 15 minutes | Cook time: 13 to 15 minutes | Serves 4

- 4 chicken breast fillets
- ¼ cup chopped ham
- ⅓ cup grated Swiss or Gruyère cheese
- ¼ cup flour
- Pinch salt
- Freshly ground black pepper, to taste
- ½ teaspoon dried marjoram
- 1 egg
- 1 cup panko bread crumbs
- Olive oil for misting

1. Preheat the air fryer to 190°C.
2. Put the chicken breast fillets on a work surface and gently press them with the palm of your hand to make them a bit thinner. Don't tear the meat.
3. In a small bowl, combine the ham and cheese. Divide this mixture among the chicken fillets. Wrap the chicken around the filling to enclose it, using Cocktail Sticks to hold the chicken together.
4. In a shallow bowl, mix the flour, salt, pepper, and marjoram. In another bowl, beat the egg. Spread the bread crumbs out on a plate.
5. Dip the chicken into the flour mixture, then into the egg, then into the bread crumbs to coat thoroughly.
6. Put the chicken in the baking pan and mist with olive oil.
7. Bake for 13 to 15 minutes or until the chicken is thoroughly cooked to 75°C. Carefully remove the Cocktail Sticks and serve.

Curried Chicken with Orange and Honey

Prep time: 10 minutes | Cook time: 16 to 19 minutes | Serves 4

- ¾ pound (340 g) boneless, skinless chicken thighs, cut into 1-inch pieces
- 1 yellow bell pepper, cut into 1½-inch pieces
- 1 small red onion, sliced
- Olive oil for misting
- ¼ cup chicken stock
- 2 tablespoons honey
- ¼ cup orange juice
- 1 tablespoon cornflour
- 2 to 3 teaspoons curry powder

1. Preheat the air fryer to 190°C.
2. Put the chicken thighs, pepper, and red onion in the baking pan and mist with olive oil.
3. Bake for 12 to 14 minutes or until the chicken is cooked to 75°C, stirring halfway through cooking time.
4. Remove the chicken and vegetables from the air fryer and set aside.
5. In a metal bowl, combine the stock, honey, orange juice, cornflour, and curry powder, and mix well. Add the chicken and vegetables, stir, and put the bowl in the air fryer.
6. Bake for 2 minutes. Remove and stir, then bake for 2 to 3 minutes or until the sauce is thickened and bubbly.
7. Serve warm.

Chili-Garlic Chicken Tenders

Prep time: 5 minutes | Cook time: 7 minutes | Serves 4

SEASONING:
- 1 teaspoon flaked salt
- ½ teaspoon garlic powder
- ½ teaspoon onion powder
- ½ teaspoon chili powder
- ¼ teaspoon sweet paprika
- ¼ teaspoon freshly ground black pepper

CHICKEN:
- 8 chicken breast tenders (1 pound / 454 g total)
- 2 tablespoons mayonnaise

1. Preheat the air fryer to 200°C.
2. For the seasoning: In a small bowl, combine the salt, garlic powder, onion powder, chili powder, paprika, and pepper.
3. For the chicken: Place the chicken in a medium bowl and add the mayonnaise. Mix well to coat all over, then sprinkle with the seasoning mix.
4. Working in batches, arrange a single layer of the chicken in the baking pan. Bake for 7 minutes, flipping halfway, until cooked through in the center. Serve immediately.

Curried Cinnamon Chicken

Prep time: 5 minutes | Cook time: 18 to 23 minutes | Serves 4

- ⅔ cup plain low-fat yogurt
- 2 tablespoons freshly squeezed lemon juice
- 2 teaspoons curry powder
- ½ teaspoon ground cinnamon
- 2 garlic cloves, minced
- 2 teaspoons olive oil
- 4 (5-ounce / 142-g) low-sodium boneless, skinless chicken breasts

1. In a medium bowl, whisk the yogurt, lemon juice, curry powder, cinnamon, garlic, and olive oil.
2. With a sharp knife, cut thin slashes into the chicken. Add it to the yogurt mixture and turn to coat. Let stand for 10 minutes at room temperature. You can also prepare this ahead of time and marinate the chicken in the refrigerator for up to 24 hours.
3. Preheat the air fryer to 180°C.
4. Remove the chicken from the marinade and shake off any excess liquid. Discard any remaining marinade. Place in the baking pan.
5. Bake the chicken for 10 minutes. With tongs, carefully turn each piece. Bake for 8 to 13 minutes more, or until the chicken reaches an internal temperature of 75°C on a meat thermometer. Serve immediately.

Chicken Lettuce Tacos with Peanut Sauce

Prep time: 10 minutes | Cook time: 6 minutes | Serves 4

- 1 pound (454 g) ground chicken
- 2 cloves garlic, minced
- ¼ cup diced onions
- ¼ teaspoon sea salt
- Cooking spray
- Peanut Sauce:
- ¼ cup creamy peanut butter, at room temperature
- 2 tablespoons tamari
- 1½ teaspoons chili sauce
- 2 tablespoons lime juice
- 2 tablespoons grated fresh ginger
- 2 tablespoons chicken broth
- 2 teaspoons sugar

FOR SERVING:

- 2 small heads butter lettuce, leaves separated
- Lime slices (optional)

1. Preheat the air fryer to 180°C. Spritz a baking pan with cooking spray.
2. Combine the ground chicken, garlic, and onions in the baking pan, then sprinkle with salt. Use a fork to break the ground chicken and combine them well.
3. Place the pan in the preheated air fryer. Bake in the preheated air fryer for 5 minutes or until the chicken is lightly browned. Stir them halfway through the cooking time.
4. Meanwhile, combine the ingredients for the sauce in a small bowl. Stir to mix well.
5. Pour the sauce in the pan of chicken, then cook for 1 more minute or until heated through.
6. Unfold the lettuce leaves on a large serving plate, then divide the chicken mixture on the lettuce leaves. Drizzle with lime juice and serve immediately.

Curried Cranberry and Apple Chicken

Prep time: 12 minutes | Cook time: 18 minutes | Serves 4

- 3 (5-ounce / 142-g) low-sodium boneless, skinless chicken breasts, cut into 1½-inch cubes
- 2 teaspoons olive oil
- 2 tablespoons cornflour
- 1 tablespoon curry powder
- 1 tart apple, chopped
- ½ cup low-sodium chicken broth
- ⅓ cup dried cranberries
- 2 tablespoons freshly squeezed orange juice
- Brown rice, cooked (optional)

1. Preheat the air fryer to 190°C.
2. In a medium bowl, mix the chicken and olive oil. Sprinkle with the cornflour and curry powder. Toss to coat. Stir in the apple and transfer to a metal pan. Bake in the air fryer for 8 minutes, stirring once during cooking.
3. Add the chicken broth, cranberries, and orange juice. Bake for about 10 minutes more, or until the sauce is slightly thickened and the chicken reaches an internal temperature of 75°C on a meat thermometer. Serve over hot cooked brown rice, if desired.

Chicken Manchurian with Ketchup Sauce

Prep time: 10 minutes | Cook time: 20 minutes | Serves 2

- 1 pound (454 g) boneless, skinless chicken breasts, cut into 1-inch pieces
- ¼ cup ketchup
- 1 tablespoon tomato-based chili sauce, such as Heinz
- 1 tablespoon soy sauce
- 1 tablespoon rice vinegar
- 2 teaspoons vegetable oil
- 1 teaspoon chili sauce, such as Tabasco
- ½ teaspoon garlic powder
- ¼ teaspoon cayenne pepper
- 2 scallions, thinly sliced
- Cooked white rice, for serving

1. Preheat the air fryer to 180°C.
2. In a bowl, combine the chicken, ketchup, chili sauce, soy sauce, vinegar, oil, chili sauce, garlic powder, cayenne, and three-quarters of the scallions and toss until evenly coated.
3. Scrape the chicken and sauce into a metal cake pan and place the pan in the air fryer. Bake until the chicken is cooked through and the sauce is reduced to a thick glaze, about 20 minutes, flipping the chicken pieces halfway through.
4. Remove the pan from the air fryer. Spoon the chicken and sauce over rice and top with the remaining scallions. Serve immediately.

Chicken and Cranberry Salad

Prep time: 10 minutes | Cook time: 6 to 10 minutes | Serves 2

- 1 pound (454 g) skinless, boneless chicken breasts
- ½ cup water
- 2 teaspoons flaked salt, plus more for seasoning
- ½ cup mayonnaise
- 1 celery stalk, diced
- 2 tablespoons diced red onion
- ½ cup chopped dried cranberries
- ¼ cup chopped walnuts
- 1 tablespoon freshly squeezed lime juice
- ¼ shredded unpeeled organic green apple
- Freshly ground black pepper, to taste

1. Add the chicken, water, and 2 teaspoons of salt to your Instant Pot.
2. Lock the lid. Press the Pressure Cook button on the Instant Pot and cook for 6 minutes on High Pressure.
3. Once cooking is complete, use a natural pressure release for 5 minutes and then release any remaining pressure. Carefully open the lid.
4. Remove the chicken from the Instant Pot to a cutting board and let sit for 5 to 10 minutes.
5. Shred the meat, transfer to a bowl, and add ¼ cup of the cooking liquid.
6. Mix in the mayonnaise and stir until well coated. Add the celery, onion, cranberries, walnuts, lime juice, and apple. Sprinkle with the salt and pepper.
7. Serve immediately.

Chicken Puttanesca

Prep time: 10 minutes | Cook time: 9 minutes | Serves 4

- 2 (6- to 7-ounce / 170- to 198-g) boneless, skinless chicken breasts
- Salt and freshly ground black pepper, to taste
- 2 tablespoons olive oil
- 12 ounces (340 g) dry penne pasta
- 1 (14.5-ounce / 411-g) can diced tomatoes with Italian herbs, with juices
- 2½ cups store-bought chicken or vegetable broth, or homemade
- 4 oil-packed rolled anchovies with capers, plus 1 tablespoon oil from the jar
- ½ cup oil-cured black or Kalamata olives
- Pinch of red pepper flakes

1. Using kitchen paper, pat the chicken dry. Sprinkle with the salt and pepper.
2. Press the Sauté button on your Instant Pot. Add and heat the oil.
3. Add the chicken and cook for 3 minutes, or until the chicken is nicely browned on one side.
4. Stir in the penne, tomatoes, broth, anchovies and oil, olives, red pepper flakes, and pepper. Place the chicken on top.
5. Secure the lid. Select the Pressure Cook mode and set the cooking time for 6 minutes on Low Pressure.
6. When the timer beeps, do a quick pressure release. Carefully open the lid.
7. Remove the chicken from the Instant Pot to a cutting board and cut into bite-size pieces. Transfer the chicken back to the pot and stir until well mixed.
8. Lock the lid and let sit for 5 minutes, or until the liquid is thickened.
9. Serve immediately.

Chicken with Cucumber and Avocado Salad

Prep time: 10 minutes | Cook time: 20 minutes | Serves 4

- 1 tablespoon olive oil
- 1 yellow onion, chopped
- 2 chicken breasts, skinless, boneless and halved
- 1 cup chicken stock
- 1 tablespoon sweet paprika
- ½ teaspoon cinnamon powder
- Salad:
- 2 cucumbers, sliced
- 1 tomato, cubed
- 1 avocado, peeled, pitted, and cubed
- 1 tablespoon chopped Coriander

1. Press the Sauté button on the Instant Pot and heat the olive oil until it shimmers.
2. Add the onion and chicken breasts and sauté for 5 minutes, stirring occasionally, or until the onion is translucent. Stir in the chicken stock, paprika, and cinnamon powder.
3. Secure the lid. Select the Pressure Cook mode and set the cooking time for 15 minutes at High Pressure.
4. Meanwhile, toss all the ingredients for the salad in a bowl. Set aside.
5. Once cooking is complete, do a natural pressure release for 10 minutes, then release any remaining pressure. Carefully open the lid.
6. Divide the chicken breasts between four plates and serve with the salad on the side.

Garlic-Chili Chicken

Prep time: 10 minutes | Cook time: 20 minutes | Serves 4

- 2 chicken breasts, skinless, boneless and halved
- 1 cup tomato sauce
- ¼ cup sweet chili sauce
- ¼ cup chicken stock
- 4 garlic cloves, minced
- 1 tablespoon chopped basil

1. Combine all the ingredients in the Instant Pot.
2. Secure the lid. Select the Pressure Cook mode and set the cooking time for 20 minutes at High Pressure.
3. Once cooking is complete, do a natural pressure release for 10 minutes, then release any remaining pressure. Carefully open the lid.
4. Divide the chicken breasts among four plates and serve.

Cajun Chicken with Bell Peppers

Prep time: 10 minutes | Cook time: 25 minutes | Serves 4

- 2 tablespoons olive oil
- 1 yellow onion, chopped
- 2 chicken breasts, skinless, boneless and cubed
- 1 cup cubed mixed bell peppers
- 1 cup cubed tomato
- 1 cup chicken stock
- 1 teaspoon Cajun seasoning
- A pinch of cayenne pepper

1. Set your Instant Pot to Sauté and heat the olive oil until hot.
2. Add the onion and chicken cubes and brown for 5 minutes. Stir in the remaining ingredients.
3. Secure the lid. Select the Pressure Cook mode and set the cooking time for 20 minutes at High Pressure.
4. Once cooking is complete, do a natural pressure release for 10 minutes, then release any remaining pressure. Carefully open the lid.
5. Serve warm.

Ground Chicken with Tomatoes

Prep time: 5 minutes | Cook time: 17 minutes | Serves 2

- 2 red bell peppers, chopped
- 1 pound (454 g) ground chicken
- 2 medium tomatoes, diced
- ½ cup chicken broth
- Salt and ground black pepper, to taste
- Cooking spray

1. Spritz a baking pan with cooking spray.
2. Set the bell pepper in the baking pan.
3. Select Broil. Set temperature to 180°C and set time to 5 minutes. Press Start to begin preheating.
4. Once preheated, place the pan into the oven. Stir the bell pepper halfway through.
5. When broiling is complete, the bell pepper should be tender.
6. Add the ground chicken and diced tomatoes in the baking pan and stir to mix well.
7. Set time to 12 minutes. Stir the mixture and mix in the chicken broth, salt and ground black pepper halfway through.
8. When cooking is complete, the chicken should be well browned.
9. Serve immediately.

Crispy Chicken Strips

Prep time: 15 minutes | Cook time: 20 minutes | Serves 4

- 1 tablespoon olive oil
- 1 pound (454 g) boneless, skinless chicken tenderloins
- 1 teaspoon salt
- ½ teaspoon freshly ground black pepper
- ½ teaspoon paprika
- ½ teaspoon garlic powder
- ½ cup whole-wheat seasoned bread crumbs
- 1 teaspoon dried parsley
- Cooking spray

1. Spray the crisper tray lightly with cooking spray.
2. Place the crisper tray on the air fry position. Select Air Fry, set the temperature to 190°C, and set the time to 20 minutes.
3. In a medium bowl, toss the chicken with the salt, pepper, paprika, and garlic powder until evenly coated.
4. Add the olive oil and toss to coat the chicken evenly.
5. In a separate, shallow bowl, mix together the bread crumbs and parsley.
6. Coat each piece of chicken evenly in the bread crumb mixture.
7. Place the chicken in the crisper tray in a single layer and spray it lightly with cooking spray. You may need to cook them in batches.
8. Air fry for 10 minutes. Flip the chicken over, lightly spray it with cooking spray, and air fry for an additional 8 to 10 minutes, until golden brown. Serve.

Chicken with Veggie Couscous Salad

Prep time: 25 minutes | Cook time: 20 minutes | Serves 4

- 3 tablespoons plus 2 teaspoons Cranberry Juice
- ½ teaspoon ground cinnamon
- 1 teaspoon minced fresh thyme
- Salt and ground black pepper, to taste
- 2 (12-ounce / 340-g) bone-in split chicken breasts, trimmed
- ¼ cup chicken broth
- ¼ cup water
- ½ cup couscous
- 1 tablespoon minced fresh parsley
- 2 ounces (57 g) cherry tomatoes, quartered
- 1 scallion, white part minced, green part sliced thin on bias
- 1 tablespoon extra-virgin olive oil
- 1 ounce (28 g) feta cheese, crumbled
- Cooking spray

1. Spritz the perforated pan with cooking spray.
2. Combine 3 tablespoons of Cranberry Juice, cinnamon, thyme, and ⅛ teaspoon of salt in a small bowl. Stir to mix well. Set aside.
3. Place the chicken breasts in the perforated pan, skin side down, and spritz with cooking spray. Sprinkle with salt and ground black pepper.
4. Select Air Fry. Set temperature to 180°C and set time to 20 minutes. Press Start to begin preheating.
5. Once preheated, place the pan into the oven. Flip the chicken and brush with Cranberry Juice mixture halfway through.
6. Meanwhile, pour the broth and water in a pot and bring to a boil over medium-high heat. Add the couscous and sprinkle with salt. Cover and simmer for 7 minutes or until the liquid is almost absorbed.
7. Combine the remaining ingredients, except for the cheese, with cooked couscous in a large bowl. Toss to mix well. Scatter with the feta cheese.
8. When cooking is complete, remove the chicken from the oven and allow to cool for 10 minutes. Serve with vegetable and couscous salad.

Chicken Thighs with Mirin

Prep time: 10 minutes | Cook time: 15 minutes | Serves 4

- ½ cup mirin
- ¼ cup dry white wine
- ½ cup soy sauce
- 1 tablespoon light Demerara sugar
- 1½ pounds (680 g) boneless, skinless chicken thighs, cut into 1½-inch pieces, fat trimmed
- 4 medium scallions, trimmed, cut into 1½-inch pieces
- Cooking spray

SPECIAL EQUIPMENT:
- 4 (4-inch) bamboo skewers, soaked in water for at least 30 minutes

1. Combine the mirin, dry white wine, soy sauce, and Demerara sugar in a saucepan. Bring to a boil over medium heat. Keep stirring.
2. Boil for another 2 minutes or until it has a thick consistency. Turn off the heat.
3. Spritz the perforated pan with cooking spray.
4. Run the bamboo skewers through the chicken pieces and scallions alternatively.
5. Arrange the skewers in the perforated pan, then brush with mirin mixture on both sides. Spritz with cooking spray.
6. Select Air Fry. Set temperature to 200°C and set time to 10 minutes. Press Start to begin preheating.
7. Once preheated, place the pan into the oven. Flip the skewers halfway through.
8. When cooking is complete, the chicken and scallions should be glossy.
9. Serve immediately.

Garlicky Whole Chicken Bake

Prep time: 10 minutes | Cook time: 1 hour | Serves 2 to 4

- ½ cup melted butter
- 3 tablespoons garlic, minced
- Salt, to taste
- 1 teaspoon ground black pepper
- 1 (1-pound / 454-g) whole chicken

1. Combine the butter with garlic, salt, and ground black pepper in a small bowl.
2. Brush the butter mixture over the whole chicken, then place the chicken in the perforated pan, skin side down.
3. Select Bake. Set temperature to 180°C and set time to 60 minutes. Press Start to begin preheating.
4. Once preheated, place the pan into the oven. Flip the chicken halfway through.
5. When cooking is complete, an instant-read thermometer inserted in the thickest part of the chicken should register at least 75°C.
6. Remove the chicken from the oven and allow to cool for 15 minutes before serving.

Coriander Chicken with Lime

Prep time: 35 minutes | Cook time: 12 minutes | Serves 4

- 4 (4-ounce / 113-g) boneless, skinless chicken breasts
- ½ cup chopped fresh Coriander
- Juice of 1 lime
- Chicken seasoning or rub, to taste
- Salt and ground black pepper, to taste
- Cooking spray

1. Put the chicken breasts in the large bowl, then add the Coriander, lime juice, chicken seasoning, salt, and black pepper. Toss to coat well.
2. Wrap the bowl in plastic and refrigerate to marinate for at least 30 minutes.
3. Preheat the air fryer to 200°C. Spritz the baking pan with cooking spray.
4. Remove the marinated chicken breasts from the bowl and place in the preheated air fryer. Spritz with cooking spray. You may need to work in batches to avoid overcrowding.
5. Bake for 12 minutes or until the internal temperature of the chicken reaches at least 75°C. Flip the breasts halfway through.
6. Serve immediately.

Garlic Chicken Wings

Prep time: 10 minutes | Cook time: 15 minutes | Serves 4

- 1 tablespoon olive oil
- 8 whole chicken wings
- Chicken seasoning or rub, to taste
- 1 teaspoon garlic powder
- Freshly ground black pepper, to taste

1. Grease the perforated pan with olive oil.
2. On a clean work surface, rub the chicken wings with chicken seasoning and rub, garlic powder, and ground black pepper.
3. Arrange the well-coated chicken wings in the perforated pan.
4. Select Air Fry. Set temperature to 200°C and set time to 15 minutes. Press Start to begin preheating.
5. Once preheated, place the pan into the oven. Flip the chicken wings halfway through.
6. When cooking is complete, the internal temperature of the chicken wings should reach at least 75°C.
7. Remove the chicken wings from the oven. Serve immediately.

Chapter 5
Fish and Seafood

Balsamic Tilapia

Prep time: 5 minutes | Cook time: 20 minutes | Serves 4

- 4 tilapia fillets, boneless
- 2 tablespoons balsamic vinegar
- 1 teaspoon avocado oil
- 1 teaspoon dried basil

1. Sprinkle the tilapia fillets with balsamic vinegar, avocado oil, and dried basil.
2. Then put the fillets in the air fryer basket or wire rack and cook at 180°C for 15 minutes.

Crunchy Red Fish

Prep time: 15 minutes | Cook time: 10 minutes | Serves 4

- 2-pound salmon fillet
- ¼ cup coconut shred
- 2 eggs, beaten
- 1 teaspoon coconut oil
- 1 teaspoon Italian seasoning

1. Cut the salmon fillet into servings.
2. Then sprinkle the fish with Italian seasonings and dip in the eggs.
3. After this, coat every salmon fillet in coconut shred and put it in the air fryer.
4. Cook the fish at 190°C for 4 minutes per side.

Cumin Catfish

Prep time: 5 minutes | Cook time: 15 minutes| Serves 4

- 1 tablespoon ground cumin
- 1 tablespoon avocado oil
- ½ teaspoon apple cider vinegar
- 1-pound catfish fillet

1. Rub the catfish fillet with ground cumin, avocado oil, and apple cider vinegar/
2. Put the fish in the air fryer and cook at 180°C for 15 minutes.

Blackened Salmon

Prep time: 15 minutes | Cook time: 10 minutes| Serves 2

- 10 oz salmon fillet
- ½ teaspoon ground coriander
- 1 teaspoon ground cumin
- 1 teaspoon dried basil
- 1 tablespoon avocado oil

1. In the shallow bowl, mix ground coriander, ground cumin, and dried basil.
2. Then coat the salmon fillet in the spices and sprinkle with avocado oil.
3. Put the fish in the air fryer basket or wire rack and cook at 395F for 4 minutes per side.

Tender Tilapia

Prep time: 5 minutes | Cook time: 20 minutes| Serves 4

- 4 tilapia fillets, boneless
- 1 tablespoon ghee
- 1 tablespoon apple cider vinegar
- 1 teaspoon dried Coriander

1. Sprinkle the tilapia fillets with apple cider vinegar and dried Coriander.
2. Put the fish in the air fryer basket or wire rack, add ghee, and cook it at 190°C for 10 minutes per side.

Rosemary Prawn Skewers

Prep time: 15 minutes | Cook time: 5 minutes| Serves 5

- 4-pounds Prawns, peeled
- 1 tablespoon dried rosemary
- 1 tablespoon avocado oil
- 1 teaspoon apple cider vinegar

1. Mix the Prawns with dried rosemary, avocado oil, and apple cider vinegar.
2. Then sting the Prawns into skewers and put in the air fryer.
3. Cook the Prawns at 200°C for 5 minutes.

Sweet Tilapia Fillets
Prep time: 5 minutes | Cook time: 14 minutes | Serves 4

- 2 tablespoons Erythritol
- 1 tablespoon apple cider vinegar
- 4 tilapia fillets, boneless
- 1 teaspoon olive oil

1. Mix apple cider vinegar with olive oil and Erythritol.
2. Then rub the tilapia fillets with the sweet mixture and put in the air fryer basket or wire rack in one layer.
3. Cook the fish at 180°C for 7 minutes per side.

Balsamic Cod
Prep time: 5 minutes | Cook time: 15 minutes | Serves 4

- 4 cod fillets, boneless
- Salt and black pepper to the taste
- 1 cup parmesan
- 4 tablespoons balsamic vinegar
- A drizzle of olive oil
- 3 spring onions, chopped

1. Season fish with salt, pepper, grease with the oil, and coat it in parmesan. Put the fillets in your air fryer's basket and cook at 190°C for 14 minutes.
2. Meanwhile, in a bowl, mix the spring onions with salt, pepper and the vinegar and whisk.
3. Divide the cod between plates, drizzle the spring onions mix all over and serve with a side salad.

Wrapped Scallops
Prep time: 15 minutes | Cook time: 7 minutes | Serves 4

- 1 teaspoon ground coriander
- ½ teaspoon ground paprika
- ¼ teaspoon salt
- 16 oz scallops
- 4 oz bacon, sliced
- 1 teaspoon sesame oil

1. Sprinkle the scallops with ground coriander, ground paprika, and salt. Then wrap the scallops in the bacon slices and secure with Cocktail Sticks.
2. Sprinkle the scallops with sesame oil.
3. Preheat the air fryer to 200°C. Put the scallops in the air fryer basket or wire rack and cook them for 7 minutes.

Cod and Sauce
Prep time: 5 minutes | Cook time: 15 minutes | Serves 2

- 2 cod fillets, boneless
- Salt and black pepper to the taste
- 1 bunch spring onions, chopped
- 3 tablespoons ghee, melted

1. In a pan that fits the air fryer, combine all the ingredients, toss gently, introduce in the air fryer and cook at 180°C for 15 minutes.
2. Divide the fish and sauce between plates and serve.

Thyme Catfish

Prep time: 10 minutes | Cook time: 12 minutes | Serves 4

- 20 oz catfish fillet (4 oz each fillet)
- 2 eggs, beaten
- 1 teaspoon dried thyme
- ½ teaspoon salt
- 1 teaspoon apple cider vinegar
- 1 teaspoon avocado oil
- ¼ teaspoon cayenne pepper
- 1/3 cup coconut flour

1. Sprinkle the catfish fillets with dried thyme, salt, apple cider vinegar, cayenne pepper, and coconut flour.
2. Then sprinkle the fish fillets with avocado oil. Preheat the air fryer to 190°C. Put the catfish fillets in the air fryer basket or wire rack and cook them for 8 minutes. Then flip the fish on another side and cook for 4 minutes more.

Salmon and Creamy Chives Sauce

Prep time: 5 minutes | Cook time: 20 minutes | Serves 4

- 4 salmon fillets, boneless
- A pinch of salt and black pepper
- ½ cup double cream
- 1 tablespoon chives, chopped
- 1 teaspoon lemon juice
- 1 teaspoon dill, chopped
- 2 garlic cloves, minced
- ¼ cup ghee, melted

1. In a bowl, mix all the ingredients except the salmon and whisk well. Arrange the salmon in a pan that fits the air fryer, drizzle the sauce all over, introduce the pan in the machine and cook at 180°C for 20 minutes.
2. Divide everything between plates and serve.

Garlic Prawn Mix

Prep time: 10 minutes | Cook time: 5 minutes | Serves 3

- 1-pound Prawns, peeled
- ½ teaspoon garlic powder
- ¼ teaspoon minced garlic
- 1 teaspoon ground cumin
- ¼ teaspoon lemon zest, grated
- ½ tablespoon avocado oil
- ½ teaspoon dried parsley

1. In the mixing bowl mix up Prawns, garlic powder, minced garlic, ground cumin, lemon zest, and dried parsley.
2. Then add avocado oil and mix up the Prawns well. Preheat the air fryer to 200°C. Put the Prawns in the preheated air fryer basket or wire rack and cook for 5 minutes.

Tilapia and Tomato Salsa

Prep time: 5 minutes | Cook time: 15 minutes | Serves 4

- 4 tilapia fillets, boneless
- 1 tablespoon olive oil
- A pinch of salt and black pepper
- 12 ounces tomatoes, chopped
- 2 tablespoons green onions, chopped
- 2 tablespoons sweet red pepper, chopped
- 1 tablespoon balsamic vinegar

1. Arrange the tilapia in a baking tray that fits the air fryer and season with salt and pepper.
2. In a bowl, combine all the other ingredients, toss and spread over the fish. Introduce the pan in the fryer and cook at 350 degrees F for 15 minutes.
3. Divide the mix between plates and serve.

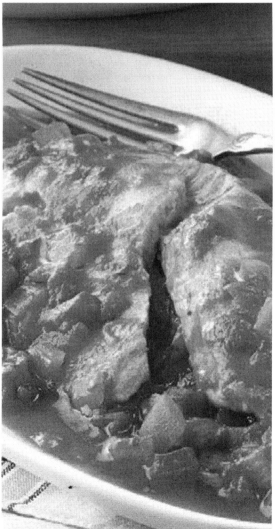

Crusted Turmeric Salmon

Prep time: 15 minutes | Cook time: 8 minutes | Serves 4

- 12 oz salmon fillet
- ¼ cup pistachios, grinded
- 1 teaspoon cream cheese
- ½ teaspoon ground nutmeg
- 2 tablespoons coconut flour
- ½ teaspoon ground turmeric
- ¼ teaspoon sage
- ½ teaspoon salt
- 1 tablespoon double cream
- Cooking spray

1. Cut the salmon fillet on 4 servings. In the mixing bowl mix up cream cheese, ground turmeric, sage, salt, and double cream.
2. Then in the separated bowl mix up coconut flour and pistachios. Dip the salmon fillets in the cream cheese mixture and then coat in the pistachio mixture.
3. Preheat the air fryer to 190°C. Place the coated salmon fillets in the air fryer and spray them with the Cooking spray .
4. Cook the fish for 8 minutes.

Catfish with Spring Onions and Avocado

Prep time: 5 minutes | Cook time: 15 minutes | Serves 4

- 2 teaspoons oregano, dried
- 2 teaspoons cumin, ground
- 2 teaspoons sweet paprika
- A pinch of salt and black pepper
- 4 catfish fillets
- 1 avocado, peeled and cubed
- ½ cup spring onions, chopped
- 2 tablespoons Coriander, chopped
- 2 teaspoons olive oil
- 2 tablespoons lemon juice

1. In a bowl, mix all the ingredients except the fish and toss.
2. Arrange this in a baking pan that fits the air fryer, top with the fish, introduce the pan in the machine and cook at 180°C for 15 minutes, flipping the fish halfway.
3. Divide between plates and serve.

Ginger Cod

Prep time: 10 minutes | Cook time: 8 minutes | Serves 2

- 10 oz cod fillet
- ½ teaspoon cayenne pepper
- ¼ teaspoon ground coriander
- ½ teaspoon ground ginger
- ½ teaspoon ground black pepper
- 1 tablespoon sunflower oil
- ½ teaspoon salt
- ½ teaspoon dried rosemary
- ½ teaspoon ground paprika

1. In the shallow bowl mix up cayenne pepper, ground coriander, ginger, ground black pepper, salt, dried rosemary, and ground paprika.
2. Then rub the cod fillet with the spice mixture. After this, sprinkle it with sunflower oil. Preheat the air fryer to 190°C. Place the cod fillet in the air fryer and cook it for 4 minutes.
3. Then carefully flip the fish on another side and cook for 4 minutes more.

Paprika Tilapia

Prep time: 5 minutes | Cook time: 20 minutes | Serves 4

- 4 tilapia fillets, boneless
- 3 tablespoons ghee, melted
- A pinch of salt and black pepper
- 2 tablespoons capers
- 1 teaspoon garlic powder
- ½ teaspoon smoked paprika
- ½ teaspoon oregano, dried
- 2 tablespoons lemon juice

1. In a bowl, mix all the ingredients except the fish and toss.
2. Arrange the fish in a pan that fits the air fryer, pour the capers mix all over, put the pan in the air fryer and cook 180°C for 20 minutes, shaking halfway.
3. Divide between plates and serve hot.

Prawn Skewers

Prep time: 10 minutes | Cook time: 5 minutes | Serves 5

- 4-pounds Prawns, peeled
- 2 tablespoons fresh Coriander, chopped
- 2 tablespoons apple cider vinegar
- 1 teaspoon ground coriander
- 1 tablespoon avocado oil
- Cooking spray

1. In the shallow bowl mix up avocado oil, ground coriander, apple cider vinegar, and fresh Coriander.
2. Then put the Prawns in the big bowl and sprinkle with avocado oil mixture. Mix them well and leave for 10 minutes to marinate. After this, string the Prawns on the skewers.
3. Preheat the air fryer to 200°C. Arrange the Prawn skewers in the air fryer and cook them for 5 minutes.

Stevia Cod

Prep time: 5 minutes | Cook time: 14 minutes | Serves 4

- 1/3 cup stevia
- 2 tablespoons coconut aminos
- 4 cod fillets, boneless
- A pinch of salt and black pepper

1. In a pan that fits the air fryer, combine all the ingredients and toss gently.
2. Introduce the pan in the fryer and cook at 350 degrees F for 14 minutes, flipping the fish halfway.
3. Divide everything between plates and serve.

Butter Crab Muffins

Prep time: 15 minutes | Cook time: 20 minutes | Serves 2

- 5 oz crab meat, chopped
- 2 eggs, beaten
- 2 tablespoons almond flour
- ¼ teaspoon baking powder
- ½ teaspoon apple cider vinegar
- ½ teaspoon ground paprika
- 1 tablespoon butter, softened
- Cooking spray

1. Grind the chopped crab meat and put it in the bowl. Add eggs, almond flour, baking powder, apple cider vinegar, ground paprika, and butter. Stir the mixture until homogenous.
2. Preheat the air fryer to 180°C. Spray the muffin molds with | Cooking spray . Then pour the crab meat batter in the muffin molds and place them in the preheated air fryer.
3. Cook the crab muffins for 20 minutes or until they are light brown. Cool the cooked muffins to the room temperature and remove from the muffin mold.

Tilapia and Kale

Prep time: 5 minutes | Cook time: 20 minutes | Serves 4

- 4 tilapia fillets, boneless
- Salt and black pepper to the taste
- 2 garlic cloves, minced
- 1 teaspoon fennel seeds
- ½ teaspoon red pepper flakes, crushed
- 1 bunch kale, chopped
- 3 tablespoons olive oil

1. In a pan that fits the fryer, combine all the ingredients, put the pan in the fryer and cook at 180°C for 20 minutes. Divide everything between plates and serve.

Chapter 6
Pork, Beef, and Lamb

Roasted Peppery Loin

Prep time: 10 minutes | Cook time: 65 minutes | Serves 3

- 3 red bell peppers
- 1½ pounds (680 g) pork loin
- 1 garlic clove, halved
- 1 teaspoon lard, melted
- ½ teaspoon cayenne pepper
- ¼ teaspoon cumin powder
- ¼ teaspoon ground bay laurel Kosher
- salt and ground black pepper, to taste

1. Roast the peppers in the preheated Air Fryer at 200°C for 10 minutes, flipping them halfway through the cooking time.
2. Let them steam for 10 minutes; then, peel the skin and discard the stems and seeds. Slice the peppers into halves and add salt to taste.
3. Rub the pork with garlic; brush with melted lard and season with spices until well coated on all sides. Place in the cooking basket and cook at 180°C for 25 minutes.
4. Turn the meat over and cook an additional 20 minutes. Serve with roasted peppers. Enjoy!

Sweet and Sour Meatballs

Prep time: 12 minutes | Cook time: 27 minutes | Serves 3

MEATBALLS:
- ½ pound (226 g) ground pork
- ¼ pound (114 g) ground turkey
- 2 tablespoons scallions, minced
- ½ teaspoon garlic, minced
- 4 tablespoons tortilla chips, crushed
- 4 tablespoons parmesan cheese, grated
- 1 egg, beaten
- Salt and red pepper, to taste

SAUCE:
- 6 ounces (170 g) jellied cranberry
- 2 ounces (57 g) chili sauce
- 2 tablespoons treacle
- 1 tablespoon wine vinegar

1. In a mixing bowl, thoroughly combine all ingredients for the meatballs. Stir to combine well and roll the mixture into 8 equal meatballs.
2. Cook in the preheated Air Fryer at 200°C for 7 minutes. Shake the air fryer basket or wire rack and continue to cook for 7 minutes longer.
3. Meanwhile, whisk the sauce ingredients in a nonstick frying pan over low heat; let it simmer, partially covered, for about 20 minutes. Fold in the prepared meatballs and serve immediately. Enjoy!

Greek-Style Pork Loin

Prep time: 20 minutes | Cook time: 50 minutes | Serves 4

- 2 pounds pork sirloin roast
- Salt and black pepper, to taste
- 1 teaspoon smoked paprika
- ½ teaspoon mustard seeds
- ½ teaspoon celery seeds
- 1 teaspoon fennel seeds
- 1 teaspoon Ancho chili powder
- 1 teaspoon turmeric powder
- ½ teaspoon ground ginger
- 2 tablespoons olive oil
- 2 cloves garlic, finely chopped
- ½ cucumber, finely chopped and squeezed
- 1 cup full-fat Greek yogurt
- 1 garlic clove, minced
- 1 tablespoon extra-virgin olive oil
- 1 teaspoon balsamic vinegar
- 1 teaspoon minced fresh dill
- A pinch of salt

1. Toss all ingredients for Greek pork in a large mixing bowl. Toss until the meat is well coated.
2. Cook in the preheated Air Fryer at 180°C for 30 minutes; turn over and cook another 20 minutes.
3. Meanwhile, prepare the tzatziki by mixing all the tzatziki ingredients. Place in your refrigerator until ready to use. Serve the pork sirloin roast with the chilled tzatziki on the side. Enjoy!

Pork Bulgogi with Peppers

Prep time: 5 minutes | Cook time: 20 minutes | Serves 2

- 2 pork loin chops
- 1 teaspoon stone-ground mustard
- 1 teaspoon cayenne pepper Kosher
- salt and ground black pepper, to taste
- 2 stalks green onion
- 1/2 teaspoon fresh ginger, grated
- 1 garlic clove, pressed
- 1 tablespoon rice wine
- 2 tablespoons gochujang chili paste
- 1 teaspoon sesame oil
- 1 tablespoon sesame seeds, lightly toasted

1. Toss the pork loin chops with the mustard, cayenne pepper, salt and black pepper. Cook in the preheated Air Fryer at 200°C for 10 minutes.
2. Check the pork chops halfway through the cooking time. Add the spring onions to the cooking basket and continue to cook for a further 5 minutes.
3. In the meantime, whisk the fresh ginger, garlic, wine, gochujang chili paste and sesame oil. Simmer the sauce for about 5 minutes until thoroughly warmed.
4. Slice the pork loin chops into bite-sized strips and top with spring onions and sauce. Garnish with sesame seeds. Enjoy!

Roasted Chinese Five-Spice Pork Ribs

Prep time: 10 minutes | Cook time: 35 minutes | Serves 3

- 2 ½ pounds (1.133 kg) country-style pork ribs
- 1 teaspoon mustard powder
- 1 teaspoon cumin powder
- 1 teaspoon shallot powder
- 1 tablespoon Five-spice powder Coarse Sea
- salt and ground black pepper
- 1 teaspoon sesame oil
- 2 tablespoons soy sauce

1. Toss the country-style pork ribs with spices and sesame oil and transfer them to the Air Fryer cooking basket.
2. Cook at 180°C for 20 minutes; flip them over and continue to cook an additional 14 to 15 minutes. Drizzle with soy sauce just before serving. Enjoy!

Roasted Boston Butt

Prep time: 10 minutes | Cook time: 32 minutes | Serves 4

- 1 pound (454 g) Boston butt, thinly sliced across the grain into
- 2-inch-long strips
- ½ teaspoon red pepper flakes, crushed Sea
- salt and ground black pepper, to taste
- ½ pound (226 g) tomatillos, chopped
- 1 small-sized onion, chopped
- 2 chili peppers, chopped
- 2 cloves garlic
- 2 tablespoons fresh Coriander, chopped
- 1 tablespoon olive oil
- 1 teaspoon sea salt

1. Rub the Boston butt with red pepper, salt, and black pepper. Spritz the bottom of the cooking basket with a nonstick cooking spray.
2. Roast the Boston butt in the preheated Air Fryer at 200°C for 10 minutes. Shake the air fryer basket or wire rack and cook another 10 minutes.
3. While the pork is roasting, make the salsa. Blend the remaining ingredients until smooth and uniform. Transfer the mixture to a saucepan and add 1 cup of water.
4. Bring to a boil; reduce the heat and simmer for 8 to 12 minutes. Serve the roasted pork with the salsa verde on the side. Enjoy!

Pork Cutlets with Plum Sauce

Prep time: 10 minutes | Cook time: 13 minutes | Serves 4

- 4 pork cutlets
- 2 teaspoon sesame oil
- ½ teaspoon ground
- black pepper Salt, to taste
- 1 tablespoon Cajun seasoning
- 2 tablespoons aged balsamic vinegar
- 2 tablespoons soy sauce
- 6 ripe plums, pitted and diced

1. Preheat your Air Fryer to 200°C. Toss the pork cutlets with the sesame oil, black pepper, salt, Cajun seasoning, vinegar, and soy sauce.
2. Transfer them to a lightly greased baking pan; lower the pan onto the cooking basket.
3. Cook for 13 minutes in the preheated Air Fryer, flipping them halfway through the cooking time. Serve warm.

Yummy Chifa Chicharonnes

Prep time: 10 minutes | Cook time: 40 minutes | Serves 4

- ½ pound (226 g) pork belly
- 2 cloves garlic, chopped
- 1 rosemary sprig, crushed
- 1 thyme sprig, crushed
- 1 teaspoon coriander
- 3 tablespoons kecap manis
- Salt and red pepper, to taste

1. Put the pork belly, rind side up, in the cooking basket; add in the garlic, rosemary, thyme and coriander.
2. Cook in the preheated Air Fryer at 180°C for 20 minutes; turn it over and cook an additional 20 minutes.
3. Turn the temperature to 200°C, rub the pork belly with the kecap manis and sprinkle with salt and red pepper. Continue to cook for 15 to 20 minutes more.
4. Let it rest on a wire rack for 10 minutes before slicing and serving. Enjoy!

Pineapple-Pork Wrap

Prep time: 15 minutes | Cook time: 60 minutes | Serves 2

- ½ pound (226 g) pork loin
- ½ teaspoon paprika Kosher
- salt and ground black pepper, to taste
- 4 ounces fresh pineapple, crushed
- ¼ cup water
- ¼ cup tomato purée
- 1 tablespoon soy sauce
- 1 teaspoon brown mustard
- 1 garlic clove, minced
- 1 shallot, minced
- 1 green chili pepper, minced
- 4 (6-inch) corn tortillas, warmed

1. Pat the pork loin dry and season it with paprika, salt and black pepper. Then, cook the pork in your Air Fryer at 180°C for 20 minutes; turn it over and cook an additional 25 minutes.
2. Then, preheat a sauté pan over a moderately high heat. Combine the pineapple, water, tomato purée, soy sauce, mustard, garlic, shallot and green chili, bringing to a rolling boil.
3. Turn the heat to simmer; continue to cook until the sauce has reduced by half, about 15 minutes. Let the pork rest for 10 minutes; then, shred the pork with two forks. Spoon the sauce over the pork and serve in corn tortillas. Enjoy!

Pork Wontons

Prep time: 10 minutes | Cook time: 8 minutes | Serves 2

- ½ pound (226 g) lean ground pork
- ½ teaspoon fresh ginger, freshly grated
- 1 teaspoon chili garlic sauce
- 1 tablespoon soy sauce
- 1 tablespoon rice wine
- ¼ teaspoon Szechuan pepper
- 2 stalks scallions, chopped
- 1 tablespoon sesame oil
- 8 (3-inch) round wonton wrappers

1. Cook the ground pork in a preheated frying pan until no longer pink, crumbling with a fork.
2. Stir in the other ingredients, except for the wonton wrappers; stir to combine well. Place the wonton wrappers on a clean work surface. Divide the pork filling between the wrappers.
3. Wet the edge of each wrapper with water, fold the top half over the bottom half and pinch the border to seal.
4. Place the pot stickers in the cooking basket and brush them with a little bit of olive oil. Cook the pot sticker at 200°C for 8 minutes. Serve immediately.

Pork Loin with Creamy Mushroom

Prep time: 5 minutes | Cook time: 3 minutes | Serves 4

- 2 pounds (907 g) top loin, boneless
- 1 tablespoon olive oil
- 1 teaspoon Celtic salt
- ¼ teaspoon ground black pepper, or more to taste
- 2 shallots, sliced
- 2 garlic cloves, minced
- 1 cup mushrooms, chopped
- 2 tablespoons plain flour
- ¾ cup cream of mushroom soup
- 1 teaspoon chili powder
- Salt, to taste

1. Pat dry the pork and drizzle with olive oil. Season with Celtic salt and pepper. Cook in the preheated Air Fryer at 190°C for 10 minutes. Top with shallot slices and cook another 10 minutes.
2. Test the temperature of the meat; it should be around 70°C. Reserve the pork and onion, keeping warm.
3. Add the cooking juices to a saucepan and preheat over medium-high heat. Cook the garlic and mushrooms until aromatic about 2 minutes. Combine the flour with the mushroom soup.
4. Add the flour mixture to the pan along with the chili powder and salt. Gradually stir into the pan. Bring to a boil; immediately turn the heat to medium and cook for 2 to 3 minutes stirring frequently. Spoon the sauce over the reserved pork and onion. Enjoy!

Spicy Pork Ribs

Prep time: 10 minutes | Cook time: 50 minutes | Serves 2

- 2 pounds St. Louis-style pork spareribs, individually cut
- 1 teaspoon seasoned salt
- ½ teaspoon ground black pepper
- 1 tablespoon sweet paprika
- ½ teaspoon mustard powder
- 2 tablespoons sesame oil
- 4 bell peppers, seeded

1. Toss and rub the spices all over the pork ribs; drizzle with 1 tablespoon of sesame oil.
2. Cook the pork ribs at 180°C for 15 minutes; flip the ribs and cook an additional 20 minutes or until they are tender inside and crisp on the outside.
3. Toss the peppers with the remaining 1 tablespoon of oil; season to taste and cook in the preheated Air Fryer at 200°C for 15 minutes.
4. Serve the warm spareribs with the roasted peppers on the side. Enjoy!

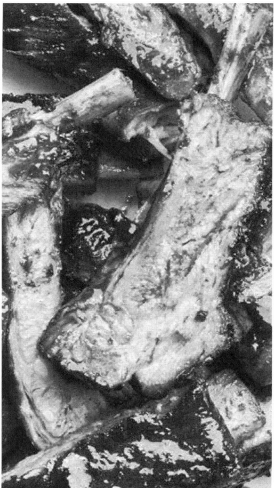

Golden and Crisp Cod Fillets

Prep time: 10 minutes | Cook time: 9 minutes | Serves 4

- 4 cod fillets
- 2 tablespoon olive oil
- 2 eggs, beaten
- 1 cup breadcrumbs
- A pinch of salt
- 1 cup flour

1. Preheat air fryer to 200°C. Mix breadcrumbs, olive oil, and a salt in a bowl. In another bowl, place the eggs. Put the flour into a third bowl. Toss the cod fillets in the flour, then in the eggs, and then in the breadcrumb mixture.
2. Place them in the greased frying basket and Air Fry for 9 minutes. At the 5-minute mark, quickly turn the fillets. Once done, remove to a plate and serve with Coriander-yogurt sauce.

Pork Chops with Applesauce

Prep time: 10 minutes | Cook time: 23 minutes | Serves 4

- 4 pork chops, bone-in Sea
- salt and ground black pepper, to taste
- ½ teaspoon onion powder
- ½ teaspoon paprika
- ½ teaspoon celery seeds
- 2 cooking apples, peeled and sliced
- 1 tablespoon honey
- 1 tablespoon groundnut oil

1. Place the pork in a lightly greased baking pan. Season with salt and pepper and transfer the pan to the cooking basket.
2. Cook in the preheated Air Fryer at 190°C for 10 minutes.
3. Meanwhile, in a saucepan, simmer the remaining ingredients over medium heat for about 8 minutes or until the apples are softened.
4. Pour the applesauce over the prepared pork chops. Add to the Air Fryer and bake for 5 minutes more. Enjoy!

Steak with Butter

Prep time: 5 minutes | Cook time: 10 minutes | Serves 6

- ½ cup olive oil
- 2 tablespoons minced garlic
- Sea salt, freshly ground black pepper, to taste
- 1½ pounds (680g) New York strip or top Rump steak
- Unsalted butter, for serving (optional)

1. In a bowl or blender, combine the olive oil, garlic, and salt and pepper to taste.
2. Place the steak in a shallow bowl or zip-top bag. Pour the marinade over the meat, seal, and marinate in the refrigerator for at least 1 hour and up to 24 hours.
3. Place a grill pan or basket in the Air fryer, set it to 200°C, and let preheat for 5 minutes.
4. Place the steak on the grill pan in a single layer, working in batches if necessary, and cook for 5 minutes. Flip the steak and cook for another 5 minutes, until an instant-read thermometer reads 50°C (or cook to your desired doneness).
5. Transfer the steak to a plate, and let rest for 10 minutes before serving. If desired, top the steaks with a pat of butter while they rest.

Steak with Bell Pepper

Prep time: 15 minutes | Cook time: 20 to 23 minutes | Serves 6

- ¼ cup avocado oil
- ¼ cup freshly squeezed lime juice
- 2 teaspoons minced garlic
- 1 tablespoon chili powder
- ½ teaspoon ground cumin
- Sea salt, Freshly ground black pepper, to taste
- 1 pound (454 g) top Rump steak or flank steak, thinly sliced against the grain
- 1 red bell pepper, cored, seeded, and cut into ½-inch slices
- 1 green bell pepper, cored, seeded, and cut into ½-inch slices
- 1 large onion, sliced

1. In a small bowl or blender, combine the avocado oil, lime juice, garlic, chili powder, cumin, and salt and pepper to taste.
2. Place the sliced steak in a zip-top bag or shallow dish. Place the bell peppers and onion in a separate zip-top bag or dish. Pour half the marinade over the steak and the other half over the vegetables. Seal both bags and let the steak and vegetables marinate in the refrigerator for at least 1 hour or up to 4 hours.
3. Line the air fryer basket or wire rack with a Air fryer liner or tin foil . Remove the vegetables from their bag or dish and shake off any excess marinade. Set the Air fryer to 200°C. Place the vegetables in the air fryer basket or wire rack and cook for 13 minutes.
4. Remove the steak from its bag or dish and shake off any excess marinade. Place the steak on top of the vegetables in the Air fryer, and cook for 7 to 10 minutes or until an instant-read thermometer reads 50°C (or cook to your desired doneness).
5. Serve with desired fixings, such as tortillas, lettuce, Soured cream, avocado slices, shredded Cheddar cheese, and Coriander.

Garlicky Beef Roast

Prep Time: 10 minutes | **Cooking Time:** 1-hour | **Servings:** 6

- 1 cup Beef Stock
- 1 tbsp. Dried basil
- 2 Sliced carrots
- 1½ lbs. Beef roast
- 2 Minced garlic cloves
- Salt and black pepper

1. In a pan, combine all the ingredients well
2. Put the pan in the Air fryer and Cook for 55 minutes at 190°C.
3. Slice the roast, share it and carrots between plates
4. Serve with cooking juices and drizzle on top

Cheesy Beef Burger with Mushroom

Prep time: 10 minutes | **Cook time:** 21 to 23 minutes | **Serves 4**

- 1 pound (454 g) minced beef, formed into 4 patties
- Sea salt, freshly ground black pepper, to taste
- 1 cup thinly sliced onion
- 8 ounces (227 g) mushrooms, sliced
- 1 tablespoon avocado oil
- 2 ounces (57 g) Gruyère cheese, shredded (about ½ cup)

1. Season the patties on both sides with salt and pepper.
2. Set the Air fryer to 190°C (190°C). Place the patties in the air fryer basket or wire rack and cook for 3 minutes. Flip and cook for another 2 minutes. Remove the burgers and set aside.
3. Place the onion and mushrooms in a medium bowl. Add the avocado oil and salt and pepper to taste; toss well.
4. Place the onion and mushrooms in the air fryer basket or wire rack. Cook for 15 minutes, stirring occasionally.
5. Spoon the onions and mushrooms over the patties. Top with the cheese. Place the patties back in the air fryer basket or wire rack and cook for another 1 to 3 minutes, until the cheese melts and an instant-read thermometer reads 70°C. Remove and let rest. The temperature will rise to 165°F (74°C), yielding a perfect medium-well burger.

Beef Steak Shallots

Prep time: 5 minutes | Cook time: 18 to 20 minutes | Serves 6

- 1½ pounds (680g) beef tenderloin steaks
- Sea salt, Freshly ground black pepper, to taste
- 4 medium shallots
- 1 teaspoon olive oil or avocado oil

1. Season both sides of the steaks with salt and pepper, and let them sit at room temperature for 45 minutes.
2. Set the Air fryer to 200°C and let it preheat for 5 minutes.
3. Working in batches if necessary, place the steaks in the air fryer basket or wire rack in a single layer and cook for 5 minutes. Flip and cook for 5 minutes longer, until an instant-read thermometer inserted in the center of the steaks registers 50°C (or as desired). Remove the steaks and tent with tin foil to rest.
4. Set the Air fryer to 150°C 150°C . In a medium bowl, toss the shallots with the oil. Place the shallots in the air fryer basket or wire rack and cook for 5 minutes, then give them a toss and cook for 3 to 5 minutes more, until crispy and golden brown.
5. Place the steaks on serving plates and arrange the shallots on top.

Steak with Horseradish Cream

Prep time: 5 minutes | Cook time: 10 minutes | Serves 8

- 2 pounds (907 g) rib eye steaks
- Sea salt, Freshly ground black pepper, to taste
- Unsalted butter, for serving
- 1 cup Soured cream
- ⅓ cup heavy (whipping) cream
- 4 tablespoons prepared horseradish
- 1 teaspoon Dijon mustard
- 1 teaspoon apple cider vinegar
- ¼ teaspoon Swerve, to taste

1. Pat the steaks dry. Season with salt and pepper and let sit at room temperature for about 45 minutes.
2. Place the grill pan in the Air fryer and set the Air fryer to 200°C. Let preheat for 5 minutes.
3. Working in batches, place the steaks in a single layer on the grill pan and cook for 5 minutes. Flip the steaks and cook for 5 minutes more, until an instant-read thermometer reads 50°C (or to your desired doneness).
4. Transfer the steaks to a plate and top each with a pat of butter. Tent with foil and let rest for 10 minutes.
5. Combine the Soured cream, double cream, horseradish, Dijon mustard, vinegar, and Swerve in a bowl. Stir until smooth.
6. Serve the steaks with the horseradish cream.

Sliced Peppery Pork

Prep time: 10 minutes | Cook time: 26 minutes | Serves 4

- 1 tablespoon olive oil
- 8 ounces (227 g) Padrón peppers
- 2 pounds (907 g) pork loin, sliced
- 1 teaspoon Celtic salt
- 1 teaspoon paprika
- 1 heaped tablespoon capers, drained
- 8 green olives, pitted and halved

1. Drizzle olive oil all over the Padrón peppers; cook them in the preheated Air Fryer at 200°C for 10 minutes, turning occasionally, until well blistered all over and tender-crisp.
2. Then, turn the temperature to 180°C.
3. Season the pork loin with salt and paprika. Add the capers and cook for 16 minutes, turning them over halfway through the cooking time.
4. Serve with olives and the reserved Padrón peppers.

Super Easy Steak for Two

Prep time: 10 minutes | Cook time: 14 minutes | Serves 2

- 1 pound (454 g) Sirloin steak, cut meat from bone in 2 pieces
- ½ teaspoon ground black pepper
- 1 teaspoon cayenne pepper
- ½ teaspoon salt
- 1 teaspoon garlic powder
- ½ teaspoon dried thyme
- ½ teaspoon dried marjoram
- 1 teaspoon Dijon mustard
- 1 tablespoon butter, melted

1. Sprinkle the Sirloin steak with all the seasonings. Spread the mustard and butter evenly over the meat.
2. Cook in the preheated Air Fryer at 200°C for 12 to 14 minutes. Taste for doneness with a meat and serve immediately.

Chapter 7
Vegan and Vegetarian

Bean, Salsa, and Cheese Tacos

Prep time: 12 minutes | Cook time: 7 minutes | Serves 4

- 1 (15-ounce / 425-g) can black beans, drained and rinsed
- ½ cup prepared salsa
- 1½ teaspoons chili powder
- 4 ounces (113 g) grated Parmesan Cheese
- 2 tablespoons minced onion
- 8 (6-inch) flour tortillas
- 2 tablespoons vegetable or extra-virgin olive oil
- Shredded lettuce, for serving

1. In a medium bowl, add the beans, salsa and chili powder. Coarsely mash them with a potato masher. Fold in the cheese and onion and stir until combined.
2. Arrange the flour tortillas on a cutting board and spoon 2 to 3 tablespoons of the filling into each tortilla. Fold the tortillas over, pressing lightly to even out the filling. Brush the tacos on one side with half the olive oil and put them, oiled side down, on the sheet pan. Brush the top side with the remaining olive oil.
3. Select Air Fry, set temperature to 200°C, and set time to 7 minutes. Select Start/Stop to begin preheating.
4. Once preheated, place the pan into the oven. Flip the tacos halfway through the cooking time.
5. Remove the pan from the oven and allow to cool for 5 minutes. Serve with the shredded lettuce on the side.

Roasted Vegetables with Basil

Prep time: 15 minutes | Cook time: 20 minutes | Serves 2

- 1 small aubergine, halved and sliced
- 1 yellow bell pepper, cut into thick strips
- 1 red bell pepper, cut into thick strips
- 2 garlic cloves, quartered
- 1 red onion, sliced
- 1 tablespoon extra-virgin olive oil
- Salt and freshly ground black pepper, to taste
- ½ cup chopped fresh basil, for garnish
- Cooking spray

1. Grease a nonstick baking dish with cooking spray.
2. Place the aubergine, bell peppers, garlic, and red onion in the greased baking dish. Drizzle with the olive oil and toss to coat well. Spritz any uncoated surfaces with cooking spray.
3. Select Bake, set temperature to 180°C, and set time to 20 minutes. Select Start/Stop to begin preheating.
4. Once preheated, place the baking dish on the bake position. Flip the vegetables halfway through the cooking time.
5. When done, remove from the oven and sprinkle with salt and pepper.
6. Sprinkle the basil on top for garnish and serve.

Balsamic Asparagus

Prep time: 15 minutes | **Cook time:** 10 minutes | **Serves 4**

- 4 tablespoons olive oil, plus more for greasing
- 4 tablespoons balsamic vinegar
- 1½ pounds (680 g) asparagus spears, trimmed
- Salt and freshly ground black pepper, to taste

1. Grease the air fry basket with olive oil.
2. In a shallow bowl, stir together the 4 tablespoons of olive oil and balsamic vinegar to make a marinade.
3. Put the asparagus spears in the bowl so they are thoroughly covered by the marinade and allow to marinate for 5 minutes.
4. Put the asparagus in the greased basket in a single layer and season with salt and pepper.
5. Select Air Fry, set temperature to 180°C, and set time to 10 minutes. Select Start/Stop to begin preheating.
6. Once preheated, place the air fry basket on the air fry position. Flip the asparagus halfway through the cooking time.
7. When done, the asparagus should be tender and lightly browned. Cool for 5 minutes before serving.

Mediterranean Baked Eggs with Spinach

Prep time: 10 minutes | **Cook time:** 10 minutes | **Serves 2**

- 2 tablespoons olive oil
- 4 eggs, whisked
- 5 ounces (142 g) fresh spinach, chopped
- 1 medium-sized tomato, chopped
- 1 teaspoon fresh lemon juice
- ½ teaspoon ground black pepper
- ½ teaspoon coarse salt
- ½ cup roughly chopped fresh basil leaves, for garnish

1. Generously grease a baking pan with olive oil.
2. Stir together the remaining ingredients except the basil leaves in the greased baking pan until well incorporated.
3. Select Bake, set temperature to 280°F (137°C), and set time to 10 minutes. Select Start/Stop to begin preheating.
4. Once preheated, place the pan on the bake position.
5. When cooking is complete, the eggs should be completely set and the vegetables should be tender. Remove from the oven and serve garnished with the fresh basil leaves.

Herbed Broccoli with Cheese

Prep time: 5 minutes | Cook time: 18 minutes | Serves 4

- 1 large-sized head broccoli, stemmed and cut into small florets
- 2½ tablespoons rapeseed oil
- 2 teaspoons dried basil
- 2 teaspoons dried rosemary
- Salt and ground black pepper, to taste
- ⅓ cup grated yellow cheese

1. Bring a pot of lightly salted water to a boil. Add the broccoli florets to the boiling water and let boil for about 3 minutes.
2. Drain the broccoli florets well and transfer to a large bowl. Add the rapeseed oil, basil, rosemary, salt, and black pepper to the bowl and toss until the broccoli is fully coated. Place the broccoli in the air fry basket.
3. Select Air Fry, set temperature to 200°C, and set time to 15 minutes. Select Start/Stop to begin preheating.
4. Once preheated, place the air fry basket on the air fry position. Stir the broccoli halfway through the cooking time.
5. When cooking is complete, the broccoli should be crisp. Remove the air fryer basket or wire rack from the oven. Serve the broccoli warm with grated cheese sprinkled on top.

Cayenne Tahini Kale

Prep time: 5 minutes | Cook time: 15 minutes | Serves 2 to 4

DRESSING:
- ¼ cup tahini
- ¼ cup fresh lemon juice
- 2 tablespoons olive oil
- 1 teaspoon sesame seeds
- ½ teaspoon garlic powder
- ¼ teaspoon cayenne pepper

KALE:
- 4 cups packed torn kale leaves (stems and ribs removed and leaves torn into palm-size pieces)
- flake salt and freshly ground black pepper, to taste

1. Make the dressing: Whisk together the tahini, lemon juice, olive oil, sesame seeds, garlic powder, and cayenne pepper in a large bowl until well mixed.
2. Add the kale and massage the dressing thoroughly all over the leaves. Sprinkle the salt and pepper to season.
3. Place the kale in the air fry basket in a single layer.
4. Select Air Fry, set temperature to 180°C, and set time to 15 minutes. Select Start/Stop to begin preheating.
5. Once preheated, place the air fry basket on the air fry position.
6. When cooking is complete, the leaves should be slightly wilted and crispy. Remove from the oven and serve on a plate.

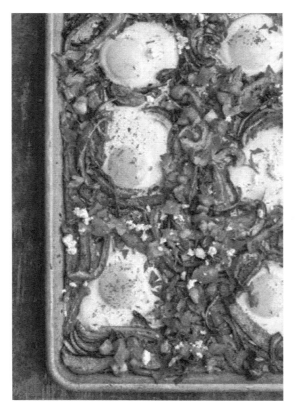

Caramelized aubergine with Yogurt Sauce

Prep time: 5 minutes | Cook time: 15 minutes | Serves 2

- 1 medium aubergine, quartered and cut crosswise into ½-inch-thick slices
- 2 tablespoons vegetable oil
- flake salt and freshly ground black pepper, to taste
- ½ cup plain yogurt (not Greek)
- 2 tablespoons harissa paste
- 1 garlic clove, grated
- 2 teaspoons honey

1. Toss the aubergine slices with the vegetable oil, salt, and pepper in a large bowl until well coated.
2. Lay the aubergine slices in the air fry basket.
3. Select Air Fry, set temperature to 200°C, and set time to 15 minutes. Select Start/Stop to begin preheating.
4. Once preheated, place the air fry basket on the air fry position. Stir the slices two to three times during cooking.
5. Meanwhile, make the yogurt sauce by whisking together the yogurt, harissa paste, and garlic in a small bowl.
6. When cooking is complete, the aubergine slices should be golden brown. Spread the yogurt sauce on a platter, and pile the aubergine slices over the top. Serve drizzled with the honey.

Cheesy Cabbage Wedges

Prep time: 5 minutes | Cook time: 20 minutes | Serves 4

- 4 tablespoons melted butter
- 1 head cabbage, cut into wedges
- 1 cup shredded Parmesan cheese
- Salt and black pepper, to taste
- ½ cup shredded Mozzarella cheese

1. Brush the melted butter over the cut sides of cabbage wedges and sprinkle both sides with the Parmesan cheese. Season with salt and pepper to taste.
2. Place the cabbage wedges in the air fry basket.
3. Select Air Fry, set temperature to 190°C, and set time to 20 minutes. Select Start/Stop to begin preheating.
4. Once preheated, place the air fry basket on the air fry position. Flip the cabbage halfway through the cooking time.
5. When cooking is complete, the cabbage wedges should be lightly browned. Transfer the cabbage wedges to a plate and serve with the Mozzarella cheese sprinkled on top.

Air Fried Winter Vegetables

Prep time: 5 minutes | Cook time: 16 minutes | Serves 2

- 1 parsnip, sliced
- 1 cup sliced butternut marrow
- 1 small red onion, cut into wedges
- ½ chopped celery stalk
- 1 tablespoon chopped fresh thyme
- 2 teaspoons olive oil
- Salt and black pepper, to taste

1. Toss all the ingredients in a large bowl until the vegetables are well coated.
2. Transfer the vegetables to the air fry basket.
3. Select Air Fry, set temperature to 190°C, and set time to 16 minutes. Select Start/Stop to begin preheating.
4. Once preheated, place the air fryer basket or wire rack on the air fry position. Stir the vegetables halfway through the cooking time.
5. When cooking is complete, the vegetables should be golden brown and tender. Remove from the oven and serve warm.

Rosemary Roasted marrow with Cheese

Prep time: 5 minutes | Cook time: 20 minutes | Serves 2

- 1 pound (454 g) butternut marrow, cut into wedges
- 2 tablespoons olive oil
- 1 tablespoon dried rosemary
- Salt, to salt
- 1 cup crumbled goat cheese
- 1 tablespoon maple syrup

1. Toss the marrow wedges with the olive oil, rosemary, and salt in a large bowl until well coated.
2. Transfer the marrow wedges to the air fry basket, spreading them out in as even a layer as possible.
3. Select Air Fry, set temperature to 180°C, and set time to 20 minutes. Select Start/Stop to begin preheating.
4. Once preheated, place the air fry basket on the air fry position.
5. After 10 minutes, remove from the oven and flip the marrow. Return the air fryer basket or wire rack to the oven and continue cooking for 10 minutes.
6. When cooking is complete, the marrow should be golden brown. Remove the air fryer basket or wire rack from the oven. Sprinkle the goat cheese on top and serve drizzled with the maple syrup.

Asian-Inspired Broccoli

Prep time: 5 minutes | Cook time: 10 minutes | Serves 2

- 12 ounces (340 g) broccoli florets
- 2 tablespoons Asian hot chili oil
- 1 teaspoon ground Sichuan peppercorns (or black pepper)
- 2 garlic cloves, finely chopped
- 1 (2-inch) piece fresh ginger, peeled and finely chopped
- flake salt and freshly ground black pepper

1. Toss the broccoli florets with the chili oil, Sichuan peppercorns, garlic, ginger, salt, and pepper in a mixing bowl until thoroughly coated.
2. Transfer the broccoli florets to the air fry basket.
3. Select Air Fry, set temperature to 190°C, and set time to 10 minutes. Select Start/Stop to begin preheating.
4. Once preheated, place the air fry basket on the air fry position. Stir the broccoli florets halfway through the cooking time.
5. When cooking is complete, the broccoli florets should be lightly browned and tender. Remove the broccoli from the oven and serve on a plate.

Roasted Brussels Sprouts with Parmesan

Prep time: 10 minutes | Cook time: 20 minutes | Serves 4

- 1 pound (454 g) fresh Brussels sprouts, trimmed
- 1 tablespoon olive oil
- ½ teaspoon salt
- ⅛ teaspoon pepper
- ¼ cup grated Parmesan cheese

1. In a large bowl, combine the Brussels sprouts with olive oil, salt, and pepper and toss until evenly coated.
2. Spread the Brussels sprouts evenly in the air fry basket.
3. Select Air Fry, set temperature to 170°C, and set time to 20 minutes. Select Start/Stop to begin preheating.
4. Once preheated, place the air fry basket on the air fry position. Stir the Brussels sprouts twice during cooking.
5. When cooking is complete, the Brussels sprouts should be golden brown and crisp. Remove the air fryer basket or wire rack from the oven. Sprinkle the grated Parmesan cheese on top and serve warm.

Creamy and Cheesy Spinach

Prep time: 10 minutes | Cook time: 15 minutes | Serves 4

- Vegetable oil spray
- 1 (10-ounce / 283-g) package frozen spinach, thawed and squeezed dry
- ½ cup chopped onion
- 2 cloves garlic, minced
- 4 ounces (113 g) cream cheese, diced
- ½ teaspoon ground nutmeg
- 1 teaspoon flaked salt
- 1 teaspoon black pepper
- ½ cup grated Parmesan cheese

1. Place the baking pan on the bake position. Select Bake, set the temperature to 180°C, and set the time to 15 minutes.
2. Spray the baking pan with vegetable oil spray.
3. In a medium bowl, combine the spinach, onion, garlic, cream cheese, nutmeg, salt, and pepper. Transfer to the prepared pan.
4. Bake for 10 minutes. Open and stir to thoroughly combine the cream cheese and spinach.
5. Sprinkle the Parmesan cheese on top. Bake for 5 minutes, or until the cheese has melted and browned.
6. Serve hot.

Mascarpone Mushrooms

Prep time: 10 minutes | Cook time: 15 minutes | Serves 4

- Vegetable oil spray
- 4 cups sliced mushrooms
- 1 medium yellow onion, chopped
- 2 cloves garlic, minced
- ¼ cup heavy whipping cream or half-and-half
- 8 ounces (227 g) mascarpone cheese
- 1 teaspoon dried thyme
- 1 teaspoon flaked salt
- 1 teaspoon black pepper
- ½ teaspoon red pepper flakes
- 4 cups cooked konjac noodles, for serving
- ½ cup grated Parmesan cheese

1. Place the baking pan on the bake position. Select Bake, set the temperature to 180°C, and set the time to 15 minutes.
2. Spray the baking pan with vegetable oil spray.
3. In a medium bowl, combine the mushrooms, onion, garlic, cream, mascarpone, thyme, salt, black pepper, and red pepper flakes. Stir to combine. Transfer the mixture to the prepared pan.
4. Bake for 15 minutes, stirring halfway through the baking time.
5. Divide the pasta among four shallow bowls. Spoon the mushroom mixture evenly over the pasta. Sprinkle with Parmesan cheese and serve.

Spicy Cauliflower Roast

Prep time: 15 minutes | Cook time: 20 minutes | Serves 4

CAULIFLOWER:
- 5 cups cauliflower florets
- 3 tablespoons vegetable oil
- ½ teaspoon ground cumin
- ½ teaspoon ground coriander
- ½ teaspoon flaked salt

SAUCE:
- ½ cup Greek yogurt or Soured cream
- ¼ cup chopped fresh Coriander
- 1 jalapeño, coarsely chopped
- 4 cloves garlic, peeled
- ½ teaspoon flaked salt
- 2 tablespoons water

1. Place the crisper tray on the roast position. Select Roast, set the temperature to 200°C, and set the time to 20 minutes.
2. In a large bowl, combine the cauliflower, oil, cumin, coriander, and salt. Toss to coat.
3. Put the cauliflower in the crisper tray. Roast for 20 minutes, stirring halfway through the roasting time.
4. Meanwhile, in a blender, combine the yogurt, Coriander, jalapeño, garlic, and salt. Blend, adding the water as needed to keep the blades moving and to thin the sauce.
5. At the end of roasting time, transfer the cauliflower to a large serving bowl. Pour the sauce over and toss gently to coat. Serve immediately.

Italian Baked Tofu

Prep time: 5 minutes | Cook time: 10 minutes | Serves 2

- 1 tablespoon soy sauce
- 1 tablespoon water
- ⅓ teaspoon garlic powder
- ⅓ teaspoon onion powder
- ⅓ teaspoon dried oregano
- ⅓ teaspoon dried basil
- Black pepper, to taste
- 6 ounces (170 g) extra firm tofu, pressed and cubed

1. In a large mixing bowl, whisk together the soy sauce, water, garlic powder, onion powder, oregano, basil, and black pepper. Add the tofu cubes, stirring to coat, and let them marinate for 10 minutes.
2. Place the baking pan on the bake position. Select Bake, set the temperature to 200°C, and set the time to 10 minutes.
3. Arrange the tofu in the baking pan. Bake for 10 minutes until crisp. Flip the tofu halfway through the cooking time.
4. Remove from the crisper tray to a plate and serve.

Crispy Tofu Sticks

Prep time: 5 minutes | Cook time: 14 minutes | Serves 4

- 2 tablespoons olive oil, divided
- ½ cup flour
- ½ cup crushed cornflakes
- Salt and black pepper, to taste
- 14 ounces (397 g) firm tofu, cut into ½-inch-thick strips

1. Grease the air fry basket with 1 tablespoon of olive oil.
2. Combine the flour, cornflakes, salt, and pepper on a plate.
3. Dredge the tofu strips in the flour mixture until they are completely coated. Transfer the tofu strips to the greased basket.
4. Drizzle the remaining 1 tablespoon of olive oil over the top of tofu strips.
5. Select Air Fry, set temperature to 180°C, and set time to 14 minutes. Select Start/Stop to begin preheating.
6. Once preheated, place the air fryer basket or wire rack on the air fry position. Flip the tofu strips halfway through the cooking time.
7. When cooking is complete, the tofu strips should be crispy. Remove from the oven and serve warm.

Tofu, Carrot and Cauliflower Rice

Prep time: 10 minutes | Cook time: 22 minutes | Serves 4

- ½ block tofu, crumbled
- 1 cup diced carrot
- ½ cup diced onions
- 2 tablespoons soy sauce
- 1 teaspoon turmeric

CAULIFLOWER:

- 3 cups cauliflower rice
- ½ cup chopped broccoli
- ½ cup frozen peas
- 2 tablespoons soy sauce
- 1 tablespoon minced ginger
- 2 garlic cloves, minced
- 1 tablespoon rice vinegar
- 1½ teaspoons toasted sesame oil

1. Place the baking pan on the roast position. Select Roast, set the temperature to 190°C, and set the time to 22 minutes.
2. Mix together the tofu, carrot, onions, soy sauce, and turmeric in the pan and stir until well incorporated.
3. Roast for 10 minutes.
4. Meanwhile, in a large bowl, combine all the ingredients for the cauliflower and toss well.
5. Remove the pan and add the cauliflower mixture to the tofu and stir to combine.
6. Return the pan to the grill and continue roasting for 12 minutes, or until the vegetables are cooked to your preference.
7. Cool for 5 minutes before serving.

Chapter 8
Rice and Grains

Cheesy Macaroni
Prep time: 5 minutes | Cook time: 15 minutes | Serves 4

- 2 cups macaroni
- 1 cup milk
- 2 cups grated Mozzarella cheese
- ½ teaspoon Italian seasoning
- Sea salt and ground black pepper, to taste
- ½ teaspoon garlic powder
- 1 teaspoon dry mustard

1. Start by preheating the air fryer to 180°C.
2. Cook the macaroni according to the package directions.
3. Drain the macaroni and place them in a lightly greased baking pan.
4. Fold in the remaining ingredients and stir to combine.
5. Place the baking pan in the corresponding position in the air fryer. Select Bake and cook the Macaroni cheese for about 15 minutes. Serve garnished with fresh Italian herbs, if desired.
6. Bon appétit!

Curry Basmati Rice
Prep time: 10 minutes | Cook time: 10 minutes | Serves 4

- 3 tablespoons olive oil
- 3 cloves garlic, chopped
- 1 large onion, peeled and chopped
- 1 sprigs fresh curry leaves, chopped
- 2 cups basmati rice, cooked
- 1 teaspoon cayenne pepper
- flake salt and ground black pepper, to taste

1. Start by preheating the air fryer to 180°C.
2. Thoroughly combine all ingredients in a lightly greased baking pan. Pour 1 cup of boiling water over the rice.
3. Place the baking pan in the corresponding position in the air fryer. Select Bake and cook for about 10 minutes or until cooked through.
4. Bon appétit!

Chawal ke Pakore with Cheese
Prep time: 5 minutes | Cook time: 15 minutes | Serves 4

- 1 cup ground rice
- ½ onion, chopped
- 2 garlic cloves, minced
- 2 tablespoons butter, room temperature
- 1 teaspoon paprika
- 1 teaspoon cumin powder
- ½ cup crumbled Paneer cheese

1. Start by preheating the air fryer to 190°C.
2. Mix all ingredients until everything is well combined. Form the mixture into patties. Transfer to the crisper tray.
3. Place the crisper tray in the corresponding position in the air fryer. Select Air Fry and cook the patties for about 15 minutes or until cooked through. Turn them over halfway through the cooking time.
4. Bon appétit!3

Eggy bread
Prep time: 5 minutes | Cook time: 8 minutes | Serves 4

- 2 eggs, beaten
- ¼ cup milk
- 2 tablespoons coconut oil, room temperature
- ½ teaspoon bourbon vanilla extract
- ½ teaspoon ground cinnamon
- 4 slices bread

1. Start by preheating the air fryer to 170°C.
2. In a mixing bowl, thoroughly combine the eggs, milk, coconut oil, vanilla, and cinnamon.
3. Then dip each piece of bread into the egg mixture; place the bread slices in a lightly greased baking pan.
4. Place the baking pan in the corresponding position in the air fryer. Select Bake and cook the bread slices for about 4 minutes; turn them over and cook for a further 3 to 4 minutes. Enjoy!

Air Fried Butter Toast

Prep time: 5 minutes | Cook time: 8 minutes | Serves 3

- 2 eggs
- ½ cup milk
- 2 tablespoons butter, room temperature
- 1 teaspoon vanilla extract
- ¼ teaspoon grated nutmeg
- ½ teaspoon cinnamon powder
- 3 slices challah bread

1. Start by preheating the air fryer to 170°C.
2. In a mixing bowl, thoroughly combine the eggs, milk, butter, vanilla, nutmeg, and cinnamon.
3. Then dip each piece of bread into the egg mixture; place the bread slices in a lightly greased crisper tray.
4. Place the crisper tray in the corresponding position in the air fryer. Select Air Fry and cook the bread slices for about 4 minutes; turn them over and cook for a further 3 to 4 minutes. Enjoy!

Figs Bread Pudding

Prep time: 10 minutes | Cook time: 20 minutes | Serves 5

- 8 slices bread, cubed
- 1 cup milk
- 2 eggs, beaten
- ¼ cup Demerara sugar
- 2 ounces (57 g) dried figs, chopped
- A pinch of sea salt
- ½ teaspoon ground cinnamon
- ½ teaspoon vanilla extract

1. Place the bread in a lightly greased baking pan.
2. In a mixing bowl, thoroughly combine the remaining ingredients.
3. Pour the milk mixture over the bread cubes. Set aside for 15 minutes to soak.
4. Preheat the air fryer to 180°C.
5. Place the baking pan in the corresponding position in the air fryer. Select Bake and cook the bread pudding for about 20 minutes or until the custard is set but still a little wobbly.
6. Serve at room temperature. Bon appétit!

Rice with Scallions

Prep time: 5 minutes | Cook time: 10 minutes | Serves 4

- 2 cups jasmine rice, cooked
- 1 cup vegetable broth
- 1 teaspoon garlic powder
- ½ cup chopped scallions
- 2 tablespoons butter, room temperature
- flake salt and red pepper, to taste

1. Start by preheating the air fryer to 180°C.
2. Thoroughly combine all ingredients in a lightly greased baking pan.
3. Place the baking pan in the corresponding position in the air fryer. Select Bake and cook for about 10 minutes or until cooked through.
4. Bon appétit!

Pecans Porridge Cups

Prep time: 6 minutes | Cook time: 12 minutes | Serves 4

- 1 cup full-fat milk
- 1 cup unsweetened applesauce
- 1 egg, beaten
- ½ cup pure maple syrup
- 1 cup old-fashioned oats
- 1 teaspoon baking powder
- 1 teaspoon pure vanilla extract
- ½ teaspoon ground cinnamon
- ¼ teaspoon freshly grated nutmeg
- A pinch of flaked salt
- ½ cup chopped pecans

1. Start by preheating the air fryer to 190°C.
2. Thoroughly combine all ingredients in a mixing bowl. Spoon the mixture into lightly greased mugs.
3. Then, place the mugs in the baking pan.
4. Place the baking pan in the corresponding position in the air fryer. Select Bake and cook the Porridge for about 12 minutes.
5. Bon appétit!

Juicy Quinoa Porridge

Prep time: 10 minutes | Cook time: 12 minutes | Serves 4

- ½ cup old-fashioned oats
- ½ cup quinoa flakes
- ¼ cup chopped almonds
- ¼ cup chopped pecans
- 2 cups orange juice
- 4 tablespoons honey
- 2 tablespoons coconut oil
- 4 tablespoons chopped dried apricots

1. Start by preheating the air fryer to 190°C.
2. Thoroughly combine all ingredients in a mixing bowl. Spoon the mixture into lightly greased mugs.
3. Then, place the mugs in the baking pan.
4. Place the baking pan in the corresponding position in the air fryer. Select Bake and cook the porridge for about 12 minutes.
5. Serve immediately. Bon appétit!

Rice Cheese Casserole

Prep time: 10 minutes | Cook time: 10 minutes | Serves 4

- 1 small shallot, minced
- 2 garlic cloves, minced
- 2 tablespoons olive oil
- ½ teaspoon paprika
- 2 eggs, whisked
- 1 cup half-and-half
- 1 cup shredded Cheddar cheese
- 2 cups cooked brown rice
- 1 tablespoon chopped Italian parsley leaves
- 1 cup cream of celery soup
- Sea salt and freshly ground black pepper, to taste

1. Start by preheating the air fryer to 180°C .
2. Thoroughly combine all ingredients in a lightly greased baking pan.
3. Place the baking pan in the corresponding position in the air fryer. Select Bake and cook for about 10 minutes or until cooked through.
4. Bon appétit!

Methi and Ragi Fritters

Prep time: 8 minutes | Cook time: 15 minutes | Serves 4

- ½ cup ground rice
- ½ cup Ragi
- ½ teaspoon baking powder
- 1 cup chopped methi
- 1 green chilli, finely chopped
- 1 teaspoon ginger-garlic paste
- 2 tablespoons sesame oil
- Sea salt and ground black pepper, to taste

1. Start by preheating the air fryer to 190°C.
2. Mix all ingredients until everything is well combined. Form the mixture into patties. Transfer to the crisper tray.
3. Place the crisper tray in the corresponding position in the air fryer. Select Air Fry and cook the patties for about 15 minutes or until cooked through. Turn them over halfway through the cooking time.
4. Bon appétit!

Doughnut Bread Pudding

Prep time: 8 minutes | Cook time: 20 minutes | Serves 6

- 2 cups diced doughnuts
- 2 eggs, whisked
- 1 cup milk
- 1 cup half-and-half
- 4 tablespoons honey
- 1 teaspoon vanilla extract
- A pinch of salt
- A pinch of grated nutmeg

1. Place the doughnuts in a lightly greased baking pan.
2. In a mixing bowl, thoroughly combine the remaining ingredients.
3. Pour the custard mixture over the doughnuts. Set aside for 15 minutes to soak.
4. Preheat the air fryer to 180°C.
5. Place the baking pan in the corresponding position in the air fryer. Select Bake and cook the bread pudding for about 20 minutes or until the custard is set but still a little wobbly.
6. Serve at room temperature. Bon appétit!

Biryani with Butter

Prep time: 5 minutes | Cook time: 10 minutes | Serves 4

- 2 cups jasmine rice, cooked
- 1 cup water
- 1 teaspoon ginger-garlic paste
- 2 tablespoons chopped shallots
- ½ teaspoon ground cinnamon
- 2 tablespoons butter
- ½ teaspoon cumin seeds
- 1 teaspoon garam masala
- ½ teaspoon turmeric powder

1. Start by preheating the air fryer to 180°C.
2. Thoroughly combine all ingredients in a lightly greased baking pan.
3. Place the baking pan in the corresponding position in the air fryer. Select Bake and cook for about 10 minutes or until cooked through.
4. Bon appétit!

Chocolate Chips Honey Muffins

Prep time: 5 minutes | Cook time: 15 minutes | Serves 6

- ½ cup plain flour
- ⅓ cup almond flour
- 1 teaspoon baking powder
- A pinch of sea salt
- A pinch of grated nutmeg
- 1 egg
- ¼ cup honey
- ¼ cup milk
- 1 teaspoon vanilla extract
- 4 tablespoons coconut oil
- ½ cup dark chocolate chips

1. Start by preheating the air fryer to 160°C.
2. Mix all ingredients in a bowl. Scrape the batter into silicone baking molds; place them in the baking pan.
3. Place the baking pan in the corresponding position in the air fryer. Select Bake and cook the muffins for about 15 minutes or until a tester comes out dry and clean.
4. Allow the muffins to cool before unmolding and serving. Bon appétit!

Baked Rolls with Cheese

Prep time: 5 minutes | Cook time: 10 minutes | Serves 4

- 1 (8-ounce / 227-g) can refrigerated crescent rolls
- 4 ounces (113 g) cream cheese, room temperature

1. Start by preheating the air fryer to 150°C.
2. Separate the dough into rectangles. Spread each rectangle with cream cheese and roll them up.
3. Place the rolls in the baking pan.
4. Place the baking pan in the corresponding position in the air fryer. Select Bake and cook the rolls for about 5 minutes; turn them over and cook for another 5 minutes.
5. Bon appétit!

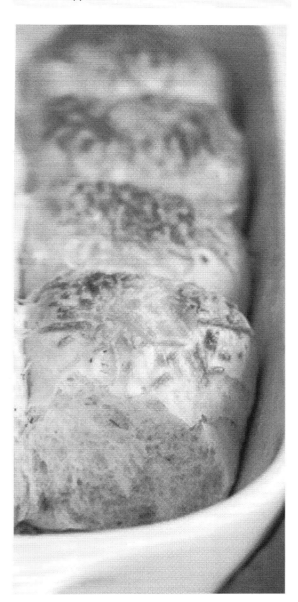

Almonds Porridge

Prep time: 5 minutes | Cook time: 12 minutes | Serves 4

- 1 cup rolled oats
- 1 cup water
- 1 cup milk
- 1 teaspoon vanilla paste
- A pinch of flaked salt
- ½ teaspoon ground cloves
- 4 tablespoons honey
- ½ cup slivered almonds

1. Start by preheating the air fryer to 190°C.
2. Thoroughly combine all ingredients in a mixing bowl. Spoon the mixture into lightly greased ramekins.
3. Then, place the ramekins in the baking pan.
4. Place the baking pan in the corresponding position in the air fryer. Select Bake and cook the Porridge for about 12 minutes. Serve warm or at room temperature.
5. Bon appétit!

Chocolate Chips muesli

Prep time: 10 minutes | Cook time: 15 minutes | Serves 8

- ½ cup old-fashioned oats
- ¼ cup unsweetened coconut flakes
- ¼ cup quinoa flakes
- ¼ cup slivered almonds
- ¼ cup chopped hazelnuts
- ¼ cup chia seeds
- 1 teaspoon ground cinnamon
- A pinch of grated nutmeg
- A pinch of sea salt
- 2 tablespoons coconut oil
- ¼ cup maple syrup
- 1 teaspoon vanilla extract
- ½ cup chocolate chips

1. Start by preheating the air fryer to 180°C.
2. Thoroughly combine all ingredients in a lightly greased baking pan.
3. Place the baking pan in the corresponding position in the air fryer. Select Bake and cook the muesli for about 15 minutes, stirring every 5 minutes.
4. Store at room temperature in an airtight container for up to three weeks.
5. Bon appétit!

Cheesy Butter Macaroni

Prep time: 5 minutes | Cook time: 15 minutes | Serves 4

- 1 cups macaroni
- 1 cup cream of onion soup
- 2 tablespoons butter
- 4 ounces (113 g) Ricotta cheese
- 6 ounces (170 g) Mozzarella cheese, crumbled
- flake salt and ground white pepper, to taste
- ½ teaspoon ground cumin
- 1 teaspoon dry mustard
- 1 teaspoon red chili powder

1. Start by preheating the air fryer to 180°C.
2. Cook the macaroni according to the package directions.
3. Drain the macaroni and place them in a lightly greased baking pan.
4. Fold in the remaining ingredients and stir to combine.
5. Place the baking pan in the corresponding position in the air fryer. Select Bake and cook the Macaroni cheese for about 15 minutes. Serve garnished with fresh Italian herbs, if desired.
6. Bon appétit!

Blueberry Cheese Rolls

Prep time: 5 minutes | Cook time: 10 minutes | Serves 6

- 1 (8-ounce / 227-g) can refrigerated crescent dinner rolls
- 6 ounces (170 g) cream cheese, room temperature
- 4 tablespoons granulated sugar
- 1 teaspoon grated lemon zest
- 1 cup fresh blueberries
- 1 cup icing sugar
- ¼ teaspoon ground cinnamon

1. Start by preheating the air fryer to 150°C.
2. Separate the dough into rectangles. Mix the remaining ingredients until well combined.
3. Spread each rectangle with the cheese mixture; roll them up tightly.
4. Place the rolls in the baking pan.
5. Place the baking pan in the corresponding position in the air fryer. Select Bake and cook the rolls for about 5 minutes; turn them over and bake for a further 5 minutes.
6. Bon appétit!

Pumpkin Porridge with Chocolate

Prep time: 5 minutes | Cook time: 12 minutes | Serves 5

- ½ cup old-fashioned oats
- ½ cup quinoa flakes
- ¼ cup chopped pecans
- 2 tablespoons ground chia seeds
- 2 tablespoons ground flax seeds
- 1 teaspoon vanilla essence
- 2 ounces (57 g) dark chocolate chips
- ½ cup tinned pumpkin
- ½ cup almond milk

1. Start by preheating the air fryer to 190°C.
2. Thoroughly combine all ingredients in a mixing bowl. Spoon the mixture into a lightly greased baking pan.
3. Place the baking pan in the corresponding position in the air fryer. Select Bake and cook the porridge for about 12 minutes.
4. Serve immediately. Bon appétit!

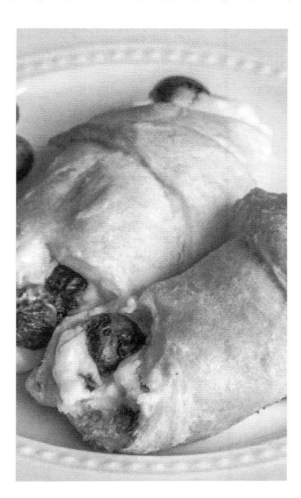

Chapter 9
Starters and Snacks

Avocado Chips

Prep time: 15 minutes | Cook time: 10 minutes | Serves 4

- 1 egg
- 1 tablespoon lime juice
- ⅛ teaspoon chili sauce
- 2 tablespoons flour
- ¾ cup panko bread crumbs
- ¼ cup cornmeal
- ¼ teaspoon salt
- 1 large avocado, pitted, peeled, and cut into ½-inch slices
- Cooking spray

1. Whisk together the egg, lime juice, and chili sauce in a small bowl.
2. On a sheet of wax paper, place the flour. In a separate sheet of wax paper, combine the bread crumbs, cornmeal, and salt.
3. Dredge the avocado slices one at a time in the flour, then in the egg mixture, finally roll them in the bread crumb mixture to coat well.
4. Place the breaded avocado slices in the air flow racks and mist them with cooking spray.
5. Slide the racks into the air fryer. Press the Power Button. Cook at 200°C for 10 minutes.
6. When cooking is complete, the slices should be nicely browned and crispy. Transfer the avocado slices to a plate and serve.

Baked Sardines with Tomato Sauce

Prep time: 10 minutes | Cook time: 20 minutes | Serves 4

- 2 pounds (907 g) fresh Sardines
- 3 tablespoons olive oil, divided
- 4 Roma tomatoes, peeled and chopped
- 1 small onion, sliced thinly
- Zest of 1 orange
- Sea salt and freshly ground pepper, to taste
- 2 tablespoons whole-wheat bread crumbs
- ½ cup white wine

1. Brush a sheet pan with a little olive oil. Set aside.
2. Rinse the Sardines under running water. Slit the belly, remove the spine and butterfly the fish. Set aside.
3. Heat the remaining olive oil in a large frying pan. Add the tomatoes, onion, orange zest, salt and pepper to the frying pan and simmer for 20 minutes, or until the mixture thickens and softens.
4. Place half the sauce in the bottom of the sheet pan. Arrange the Sardines on top and spread the remaining half the sauce over the fish. Sprinkle with the bread crumbs and drizzle with the white wine.
5. Slide the pan into the air fryer. Press the Power Button. Cook at 200°C for 20 minutes.
6. When cooking is complete, remove from the air fryer. Serve immediately.

Broiled Prosciutto-Wrapped Pears

Prep time: 12 minutes | Cook time: 6 minutes | Serves 8

- 2 large, ripe Anjou pears
- 4 thin slices Parma prosciutto
- 2 teaspoons aged balsamic vinegar

1. Peel the pears. Slice into 8 wedges and cut out the core from each wedge.
2. Cut the prosciutto into 8 long strips. Wrap each pear wedge with a strip of prosciutto. Place the wrapped pears in a sheet pan.
3. Slide the pan into the air fryer. Cook for 6 minutes.
4. After 2 or 3 minutes, check the pears. The pears should be turned over if the prosciutto is beginning to crisp up and brown. Return to the air fryer and continue cooking.
5. When cooking is complete, remove from the air fryer. Drizzle the pears with the balsamic vinegar and serve warm.

Browned Ricotta with Capers and Lemon

Prep time: 10 minutes | Cook time: 8 minutes | Serves 4 to 6

- 1½ cups whole milk ricotta cheese
- 2 tablespoons extra-virgin olive oil
- 2 tablespoons capers, rinsed
- Zest of 1 lemon, plus more for garnish
- 1 teaspoon finely chopped fresh rosemary
- Pinch crushed red pepper flakes
- Salt and freshly ground black pepper, to taste
- 1 tablespoon grated Parmesan cheese

1. In a mixing bowl, stir together the ricotta cheese, olive oil, capers, lemon zest, rosemary, red pepper flakes, salt, and pepper until well combined.
2. Spread the mixture evenly in a baking dish.
3. Slide the baking dish into the air fryer. Press the Power Button. Cook at 190°C for 8 minutes.
4. When cooking is complete, the top should be nicely browned. Remove from the air fryer and top with a sprinkle of grated Parmesan cheese. Garnish with the lemon zest and serve warm.

Bruschetta with Tomato and Basil

Prep time: 5 minutes | Cook time: 3 minutes | Serves 6

- 4 tomatoes, diced
- ⅓ cup shredded fresh basil
- ¼ cup shredded Parmesan cheese
- 1 tablespoon balsamic vinegar
- 1 tablespoon minced garlic
- 1 teaspoon olive oil
- 1 teaspoon salt
- 1 teaspoon freshly ground black pepper
- 1 loaf French bread, cut into 1-inch-thick slices
- Cooking spray

1. Mix the tomatoes and basil in a medium bowl. Add the cheese, vinegar, garlic, olive oil, salt, and pepper and stir until well incorporated. Set aside.
2. Spritz the air flow racks with cooking spray and lay the bread slices in the racks. Spray the slices with cooking spray.
3. Slide the racks into the air fryer. Press the Power Button. Cook at 120°C for 3 minutes.
4. When cooking is complete, remove from the air fryer to a plate. Top each slice with a generous spoonful of the tomato mixture and serve.

Roasted Grapes with Yogurt

Prep time: 5 minutes | Cook time: 10 minutes | Serves 6

- 2 cups seedless red grapes, rinsed and patted dry
- 1 tablespoon apple cider vinegar
- 1 tablespoon honey
- 1 cup low-fat Greek yogurt
- 2 tablespoons 2 percent milk
- 2 tablespoons minced fresh basil

1. Spread the red grapes in the air flow racks and drizzle with the cider vinegar and honey. Lightly toss to coat.
2. Slide the racks into the air fryer. Press the Power Button. Cook at 190°C for 10 minutes.
3. When cooking is complete, the grapes will be wilted but still soft. Remove from the air fryer.
4. In a medium bowl, whisk together the yogurt and milk. Gently fold in the grapes and basil.
5. Serve immediately.

Roasted Mixed Nuts

Prep time: 5 minutes | Cook time: 20 minutes | Serves 6

- 2 cups mixed nuts (walnuts, pecans, and almonds)
- 2 tablespoons egg white
- 2 tablespoons sugar
- 1 teaspoon paprika
- 1 teaspoon ground cinnamon
- Cooking spray

1. Line the air flow racks with greaseproof paper and spray with cooking spray.
2. Stir together the mixed nuts, egg white, sugar, paprika, and cinnamon in a small bowl until the nuts are fully coated. Place the nuts in the air flow racks.
3. Slide the racks into the air fryer. Press the Power Button. Cook at 150°C for 20 minutes.
4. Stir the nuts halfway through the cooking time.
5. When cooking is complete, remove from the air fryer. Transfer the nuts to a bowl and serve warm.

Salty Baked Almonds

Prep time: 5 minutes | Cook time: 25 minutes | Serves 4

- 1 cup raw almonds
- 1 egg white, beaten
- ½ teaspoon coarse sea salt

1. Spread the almonds on the sheet pan in an even layer.
2. Slide the pan into the air fryer. Press the Power Button. Cook at 180°C for 20 minutes.
3. When cooking is complete, the almonds should be lightly browned and fragrant. Remove from the air fryer.
4. Coat the almonds with the egg white and sprinkle with the salt. Return the pan back to the air fryer.
5. Press the Power Button. Cook at 180°C for 5 minutes.
6. When cooking is complete, the almonds should be dried. Cool completely before serving.

Banger and Mushroom Empanadas

Prep time: 5 minutes | Cook time: 12 minutes | Serves 4

- ½ pound (227 g) Kielbasa smoked banger, chopped
- 4 chopped tinned mushrooms
- 2 tablespoons chopped onion
- ½ teaspoon ground cumin
- ¼ teaspoon paprika
- Salt and black pepper, to taste
- ½ package puff pastry dough, at room temperature
- 1 egg, beaten
- Cooking spray

1. Combine the banger, mushrooms, onion, cumin, paprika, salt, and pepper in a bowl and stir to mix well.
2. Make the empanadas: Place the puff pastry dough on a lightly floured surface. Cut circles into the dough with a glass. Place 1 tablespoon of the banger mixture into the center of each pastry circle. Fold each in half and pinch the edges to seal. Using a fork, crimp the edges. Brush them with the beaten egg and mist with cooking spray.
3. Spritz the air flow racks with cooking spray. Place the empanadas in the air flow racks.
4. Slide the racks into the air fryer. Press the Power Button. Cook at 180°C for 12 minutes.
5. Flip the empanadas halfway through the cooking time.
6. When cooking is complete, the empanadas should be golden brown. Remove from the air fryer. Allow them to cool for 5 minutes and serve hot.

Banger and Onion Rolls

Prep time: 15 minutes | Cook time: 15 minutes | Serves 12

- 1 pound (454 g) bulk breakfast banger
- ½ cup finely chopped onion
- ½ cup fresh bread crumbs
- ½ teaspoon dried mustard
- ½ teaspoon dried sage
- ¼ teaspoon cayenne pepper
- 1 large egg, beaten
- 1 garlic clove, minced
- 2 sheets (1 package) frozen puff pastry, thawed
- plain flour, for dusting

1. In a medium bowl, break up the banger. Stir in the onion, bread crumbs, mustard, sage, cayenne pepper, egg and garlic. Divide the banger mixture in half and tightly wrap each half in Cling Film. Refrigerate for 5 to 10 minutes.
2. Lay the pastry sheets on a lightly floured work surface. Using a rolling pin, lightly roll out the pastry to smooth out the dough. Take out one of the banger packages and form the banger into a long roll. Remove the Cling Film and place the banger on top of the puff pastry about 1 inch from one of the long edges. Roll the pastry around the banger and pinch the edges of the dough together to seal. Repeat with the other pastry sheet and banger.
3. Slice the logs into lengths about 1½ inches long. Place the banger rolls on a sheet pan, cut-side down.
4. Slide the pan into the air fryer. Press the Power Button. Cook at 180°C for 15 minutes.
5. After 7 or 8 minutes, rotate the pan and continue cooking.
6. When cooking is complete, the rolls will be golden brown and sizzling. Remove the pan from the air fryer and let cool for 5 minutes.

The UK Air Fryer Cookbook for beginners | 77

Banger Balls With Cheese

Prep time: 10 minutes | **Cook time:** 10 minutes | **Serves 8**

- 12 ounces (340 g) mild ground banger
- 1½ cups baking mix
- 1 cup shredded mild Cheddar cheese
- 3 ounces (85 g) cream cheese, at room temperature
- 1 to 2 tablespoons olive oil

1. Line the air flow racks with greaseproof paper. Set aside.
2. Mix the ground banger, baking mix, Cheddar cheese, and cream cheese in a large bowl and stir to incorporate.
3. Divide the banger mixture into 16 equal portions and roll them into 1-inch balls with your hands. Arrange the banger balls on the parchment, leaving space between each ball. Brush the banger balls with the olive oil.
4. Slide the racks into the air fryer. Press the Power Button. Cook at 160°C for 10 minutes.
5. Flip the balls halfway through the cooking time.
6. When cooking is complete, the balls should be firm and lightly browned on both sides. Remove from the air fryer to a plate and serve warm.

Prawn Toasts with Sesame Seeds

Prep time: 15 minutes | **Cook time:** 8 minutes | **Serves 4 to 6**

- ½ pound (227 g) raw Prawn, peeled and deveined
- 1 egg, beaten
- 2 scallions, chopped, plus more for garnish
- 2 tablespoons chopped fresh Coriander
- 2 teaspoons grated fresh ginger
- 1 to 2 teaspoons sriracha sauce
- 1 teaspoon soy sauce
- ½ teaspoon toasted sesame oil
- 6 slices thinly sliced white sandwich bread
- ½ cup sesame seeds
- Cooking spray
- Thai chili sauce, for serving

1. In a food processor, add the Prawn, egg, scallions, Coriander, ginger, sriracha sauce, soy sauce and sesame oil, and pulse until chopped finely. Stop the food processor occasionally to scrape down the sides. Transfer the Prawn mixture to a bowl.
2. On a clean work surface, cut the crusts off the sandwich bread. Using a brush, generously brush one side of each slice of bread with Prawn mixture.
3. Place the sesame seeds on a plate. Press bread slices, Prawn-side down, into sesame seeds to coat evenly. Cut each slice diagonally into quarters.
4. Spritz the air flow racks with cooking spray. Spread the coated slices in a single layer in the air flow racks.
5. Slide the racks into the air fryer. Press the Power Button. Cook at 200°C for 8 minutes.
6. Flip the bread slices halfway through.
7. When cooking is complete, they should be golden and crispy. Remove from the air fryer to a plate and let cool for 5 minutes. Top with the chopped scallions and serve warm with Thai chili sauce.

Tuna Melts with Scallions

Prep time: 10 minutes | Cook time: 6 minutes | Serves 6

- 2 (5- to 6-ounce / 142- to 170-g) cans oil-packed tuna, drained
- 1 large scallion, chopped
- 1 small stalk celery, chopped
- ⅓ cup mayonnaise
- 1 tablespoon chopped fresh dill
- 1 tablespoon capers, drained
- ¼ teaspoon celery salt
- 12 slices cocktail rye bread
- 2 tablespoons butter, melted
- 6 slices sharp Cheddar cheese

1. In a medium bowl, stir together the tuna, scallion, celery, mayonnaise, dill, capers and celery salt.
2. Brush one side of the bread slices with the butter. Arrange the bread slices on a sheet pan, buttered-side down. Scoop a heaping tablespoon of the tuna mixture on each slice of bread, spreading it out even to the edges.
3. Cut the cheese slices to fit the dimensions of the bread and place a cheese slice on each piece.
4. Slide the pan into the air fryer. Press the Power Button. Cook at 190°C for 6 minutes.
5. After 4 minutes, remove from the air fryer and check the tuna melts. The tuna melts are done when the cheese has melted and the tuna is heated through. If needed, continue cooking.
6. When cooking is complete, remove from the air fryer. Use a spatula to transfer the tuna melts to a clean work surface and slice each one in half diagonally. Serve warm.

Turkey Bacon-Wrapped Dates

Prep time: 10 minutes | Cook time: 6 minutes | Makes 16 Starters

- 16 whole dates, pitted
- 16 whole almonds
- 6 to 8 strips turkey bacon, cut in half

SPECIAL EQUIPMENT:
- 16 Cocktail Sticks, soaked in water for at least 30 minutes

1. On a flat work surface, stuff each pitted date with a whole almond.
2. Wrap half slice of bacon around each date and secure it with a toothpick.
3. Place the bacon-wrapped dates in the air flow racks.
4. Slide the racks into the air fryer. Press the Power Button. Cook at 200°C for 6 minutes.
5. When cooking is complete, transfer the dates to a paper towel-lined plate to drain. Serve hot.

Lemon Ricotta Cake

Prep time: 5 minutes | Cook time: 25 minutes | Serves 6

- 17.5 ounces (496 g) ricotta cheese
- 5.4 ounces (153 g) sugar
- 3 eggs, beaten
- 3 tablespoons flour
- 1 lemon, juiced and zested
- 2 teaspoons vanilla extract

1. In a large mixing bowl, stir together all the ingredients until the mixture reaches a creamy consistency.
2. Pour the mixture into a baking pan and place in the air fryer.
3. Slide the pan into the air fryer. Press the Power Button. Cook at 160°C for 25 minutes.
4. When cooking is complete, a toothpick inserted in the center should come out clean.
5. Allow to cool for 10 minutes on a wire rack before serving.

Lemon-Butter Shortbread

Prep time: 10 minutes | Cook time: 36 to 40 minutes | Makes 4 dozen biscuits

- 1 tablespoon grated lemon zest
- 1 cup granulated sugar
- 1 pound (454 g) unsalted butter, at room temperature
- ¼ teaspoon fine salt
- 4 cups plain flour
- ⅓ cup cornflour
- Cooking spray

1. Add the lemon zest and sugar to a stand mixer fitted with the paddle attachment and beat on medium speed for 1 to 2 minute. Let stand for about 5 minutes. Fold in the butter and salt and blend until fluffy.
2. Mix the flour and cornflour in a large bowl. Add to the butter mixture and mix to combine.
3. Spritz a sheet pan with cooking spray and spread a piece of greaseproof paper onto the pan. Scrape the dough into the pan until even and smooth.
4. Slide the pan into the air fryer. Press the Power Button. Cook at 160°C for 36 minutes.
5. After 20 minutes, check the shortbread, rotating the pan if it is not browning evenly. Continue cooking for another 16 minutes until lightly browned.
6. When done, remove from the air fryer. Slice and allow to cool for 5 minutes before serving.

Lemon-Raspberry Muffins

Prep time: 5 minutes | Cook time: 15 minutes | Serves 6

- 2 cups almond flour
- ¾ cup Swerve
- 1¼ teaspoons baking powder
- ⅓ teaspoon ground allspice
- ⅓ teaspoon ground anise star
- ½ teaspoon grated lemon zest
- ¼ teaspoon salt
- 2 eggs
- 1 cup Soured cream
- ½ cup coconut oil
- ½ cup raspberries

1. Line a muffin pan with 6 paper liners.
2. In a mixing bowl, mix the almond flour, Swerve, baking powder, allspice, anise, lemon zest, and salt.
3. In another mixing bowl, beat the eggs, Soured cream, and coconut oil until well mixed. Add the egg mixture to the flour mixture and stir to combine. Mix in the raspberries.
4. Scrape the batter into the prepared muffin cups, filling each about three-quarters full.
5. Slide the pan into the air fryer. Press the Power Button. Cook at 345°F (174°C) for 15 minutes.
6. When cooking is complete, the tops should be golden and a toothpick inserted in the middle should come out clean.
7. Allow the muffins to cool for 10 minutes in the muffin pan before removing and serving.

Mixed Berries with Pecan Streusel Topping

Prep time: 5 minutes | Cook time: 17 minutes | Serves 3

- ½ cup mixed berries
- Cooking spray
- Topping:
- 1 egg, beaten
- 3 tablespoons almonds, slivered
- 3 tablespoons chopped pecans
- 2 tablespoons chopped walnuts
- 3 tablespoons granulated Swerve
- 2 tablespoons cold salted butter, cut into pieces
- ½ teaspoon ground cinnamon

1. Lightly spray a baking dish with cooking spray.
2. Make the topping: In a medium bowl, stir together the beaten egg, nuts, Swerve, butter, and cinnamon until well blended.
3. Put the mixed berries in the bottom of the baking dish and spread the topping over the top.
4. Slide the baking dish into the air fryer. Press the Power Button. Cook at 170°C for 17 minutes.
5. When cooking is complete, the fruit should be bubbly and topping should be golden brown.
6. Allow to cool for 5 to 10 minutes before serving.

Orange and Anise Cake

Prep time: 5 minutes | Cook time: 20 minutes | Serves 6

- 1 stick butter, at room temperature
- 5 tablespoons liquid monk fruit
- 2 eggs plus 1 egg yolk, beaten
- ⅓ cup hazelnuts, roughly chopped
- 3 tablespoons sugar-free orange marmalade
- 6 ounces (170 g) unbleached almond flour
- 1 teaspoon baking soda
- ½ teaspoon baking powder
- ½ teaspoon ground cinnamon
- ½ teaspoon ground allspice
- ½ ground anise seed
- Cooking spray

1. Lightly spritz a baking pan with cooking spray.
2. In a mixing bowl, whisk the butter and liquid monk fruit until the mixture is pale and smooth. Mix in the beaten eggs, hazelnuts, and marmalade and whisk again until well incorporated.
3. Add the almond flour, baking soda, baking powder, cinnamon, allspice, anise seed and stir to mix well.
4. Scrape the batter into the prepared baking pan.
5. Slide the pan into the air fryer. Press the Power Button. Cook at 160°C for 20 minutes.
6. When cooking is complete, the top of the cake should spring back when gently pressed with your fingers.
7. Transfer to a wire rack and let the cake cool to room temperature. Serve immediately.

Appendix 1 Measurement Conversion Chart

Volume Equivalents (Dry)	
US STANDARD	METRIC (APPROXIMATE)
1/8 teaspoon	0.5 mL
1/4 teaspoon	1 mL
1/2 teaspoon	2 mL
3/4 teaspoon	4 mL
1 teaspoon	5 mL
1 tablespoon	15 mL
1/4 cup	59 mL
1/2 cup	118 mL
3/4 cup	177 mL
1 cup	235 mL
2 cups	475 mL
3 cups	700 mL
4 cups	1 L

Weight Equivalents	
US STANDARD	METRIC (APPROXIMATE)
1 ounce	28 g
2 ounces	57 g
5 ounces	142 g
10 ounces	284 g
15 ounces	425 g
16 ounces (1 pound)	455 g
1.5 pounds	680 g
2 pounds	907 g

Volume Equivalents (Liquid)		
US STANDARD	US STANDARD (OUNCES)	METRIC (APPROXIMATE)
2 tablespoons	1 fl.oz.	30 mL
1/4 cup	2 fl.oz.	60 mL
1/2 cup	4 fl.oz.	120 mL
1 cup	8 fl.oz.	240 mL
1 1/2 cup	12 fl.oz.	355 mL
2 cups or 1 pint	16 fl.oz.	475 mL
4 cups or 1 quart	32 fl.oz.	1 L
1 gallon	128 fl.oz.	4 L

Temperatures Equivalents	
FAHRENHEIT(F)	CELSIUS(C) APPROXIMATE)
225 °F	107 °C
250 °F	120 ° °C
275 °F	135 °C
300 °F	150 °C
325 °F	160 °C
350 °F	180 °C
375 °F	190 °C
400 °F	205 °C
425 °F	220 °C
450 °F	235 °C
475 °F	245 °C
500 °F	260 °C

Appendix 2 The Dirty Dozen and Clean Fifteen

The Environmental Working Group (EWG) is a nonprofit, nonpartisan organization dedicated to protecting human health and the environment Its mission is to empower people to live healthier lives in a healthier environment. This organization publishes an annual list of the twelve kinds of produce, in sequence, that have the highest amount of pesticide residue-the Dirty Dozen-as well as a list of the fifteen kinds ofproduce that have the least amount of pesticide residue-the Clean Fifteen.

THE DIRTY DOZEN	
The 2016 Dirty Dozen includes the following produce. These are considered among the year's most important produce to buy organic:	
Strawberries	Spinach
Apples	Tomatoes
Nectarines	Bell peppers
Peaches	Cherry tomatoes
Celery	Cucumbers
Grapes	Kale/collard greens
Cherries	Hot peppers

The Dirty Dozen list contains two additional itemskale/collard greens and hot peppers-because they tend to contain trace levels of highly hazardous pesticides.

THE CLEAN FIFTEEN	
The least critical to buy organically are the Clean Fifteen list. The following are on the 2016 list:	
Avocados	Papayas
Corn	Kiw
Pineapples	Eggplant
Cabbage	Honeydew
Sweet peas	Grapefruit
Onions	Cantaloupe
Asparagus	Cauliflower
Mangos	

Some of the sweet corn sold in the United States are made from genetically engineered (GE) seedstock. Buy organic varieties of these crops to avoid GE produce.

Appendix 3 Index

A

Air Fried Butter Toast	64
Air Fried Winter Vegetables	56
Air-Fried Hard-Boiled Eggs	8
Almonds Porridge	69
Asian-Inspired Broccoli	57
Avocado Chips	73

B

Baked Rolls with Cheese	69
Baked Sardines with Tomato Sauce	73
Balsamic Asparagus	53
Balsamic Cod	33
Balsamic Tilapia	31
Banger and Mushroom Empanadas	77
banger and Onion Rolls	77
Banger Balls With Cheese	78
banger Eggs with Smoky Mustard Sauce	18
Bean, Salsa, and Cheese Tacos	52
Beef Steak Shallots	49
Biryani with Butter	68
Blackened Salmon	32
Blueberry Cheese Rolls	71
Broiled Prosciutto-Wrapped Pears	74
Browned Ricotta with Capers and Lemon	74
Bruschetta with Tomato and Basil	75
Butter Crab Muffins	38

C

Cajun Chicken with Bell Peppers	26
Caramelized aubergine with Yogurt Sauce	55
Catfish with Spring Onions and Avocado	36
Cayenne Tahini Kale	54
Chawal ke Pakore with Cheese	63
Cheddar banger Meatball	14
Cheesy Beef Burger with Mushroom	48
Cheesy Butter Macaroni	70
Cheesy Cabbage Wedges	55
Cheesy Macaroni	62
Chicken and Bell Pepper Fajitas	20
Chicken and Cranberry Salad	24
Chicken Cordon Bleu with Emmethaler	20
Chicken Lettuce Tacos with Peanut Sauce	22
Chicken Manchurian with Ketchup Sauce	23
Chicken Nuggets with Almond Crust	20
Chicken Puttanesca	24
Chicken Thighs with Mirin	28
Chicken with Cucumber and Avocado Salad	25
Chicken with Veggie Couscous Salad	27
Chili Taco Seasoning	6
Chili-Garlic Chicken Tenders	21
Chocolate Chips Honey Muffins	68
Chocolate Chips muesli	70
Classic Marinara Sauce	10
Classic Ranch Dressing	7
Cod and Sauce	33
Coriander Chicken with Lime	29

C (continued)

Creamy Almond Glaze	6
Creamy and Cheesy Spinach	58
Creamy Blue Cheese Dressing	7
Crispy Chicken Strips	27
Crispy Tofu Sticks	60
Crunchy Red Fish	31
Crusted Turmeric Salmon	36
Cumin Catfish	32
Curried Chicken with Orange and Honey	21
Curried Cinnamon Chicken	22
Curried Cranberry and Apple Chicken	23
Curry Basmati Rice	62

D

Dijon Mayonnaise	9
Doughnut Bread Pudding	67

E

Easy Pizza Dough	7
Eggy bread	63
Enchilada Sauce	10

F

Figs Bread Pudding	64

G

Garlic Chicken Wings	29
Garlic Prawn Mix	35
Garlic-Chili Chicken	25
Garlicky banger Gravy	6
Garlicky Beef Roast	48
Garlicky Whole Chicken Bake	28
Ginger Cod	37
Golden and Crisp Cod Fillets	46
Greek-Style Pork Loin	41
Ground Chicken with Tomatoes	26

H

Herb-Avocado Compound Butter	8
Herbed Broccoli with Cheese	54
Homemade Tzatziki Sauce	7

I

Italian Baked Tofu	59

J

Juicy Quinoa Porridge	66

L

Lean Turkey banger	13
Lemon Ricotta Cake	80
Lemon-Butter Shortbread	80
Lemon-Raspberry Muffins	81
Lemony Caesar Dressing	9
Lime Basil Dressing	9

M

Mascarpone Mushrooms	58
Mediterranean Baked Eggs with Spinach	53
Methi and Ragi Fritters	67
Mixed Berries with Pecan Streusel Topping	81
Muffins with Pecans and Kiwi	17

N

Nutty muesli	18

O

Orange and Anise Cake	81
Oregano Balsamic Dressing	8

P

Paprika Tilapia	37
Pecans Porridge Cups	65
Pineapple-Pork Wrap	44
Pork banger Cheese Biscuit	15
Pork banger Egg Cup	14
Pork Bulgogi with Peppers	41
Pork Chops with Applesauce	46
Pork Cutlets with Plum Sauce	43
Pork Loin with Creamy Mushroom	45
Pork Wontons	44
Prawn Skewers	38
Prawn Toasts with Sesame Seeds	78
Pumpkin Porridge with Chocolate	71

R

Rice Cheese Casserole	66
Rice with Scallions	65
Roasted Boston Butt	42
Roasted Brussels Sprouts with Parmesan	57
Roasted Chinese Five-Spice Pork Ribs	42
Roasted Grapes with Yogurt	75
Roasted Mixed Nuts	76
Roasted Mushrooms	11
Roasted Peppery Loin	40
Roasted Vegetables with Basil	52
Roma Tomato and Spinach Egg	13
Rosemary Prawn Skewers	32
Rosemary Roasted marrow with Cheese	56

S

Salmon and Creamy Chives Sauce	34
Salty Baked Almonds	76
Savory Mozzarella Bagels	14
Shawarma Spice Mix	11
Simple Teriyaki Sauce	11
Sliced Peppery Pork	50
Soft Pita Breads	16
Speedy Omelet	15
Spicy Cauliflower Roast	59
Spicy Pork Ribs	45
Steak with Bell Pepper	47
Steak with Butter	47
Steak with Horseradish Cream	49
Stevia Cod	38
Strawberry-Coconut Butter	8
Super Easy Steak for Two	50
Sweet and Sour Meatballs	40

Sweet Tilapia Fillets	33

T

Tartar Sauce	6
Tender Tilapia	32
Thyme Catfish	34
Tilapia and Kale	38
Tilapia and Tomato Salsa	35
Tofu, Carrot and Cauliflower Rice	60
Tomato-Avocado Toast	16
Tuna Melts with Scallions	79
Turkey Bacon-Wrapped Dates	79
Turkey banger Burger with Avocado	15
Turkey-Mushroom Burger	17

V

Vegan Sandwich-Tofu with Cabbage	17

W

Wrapped Scallops	33

Y

Yummy Chifa Chicharonnes	43

IRENE M. BASS

Printed in Great Britain
by Amazon